How to Teach Art to Children

is designed to increase student awareness of the different kinds of art. It gives students a wide range of experiences and helps them to appreciate the art around them. Most importantly, it lets them know that there is no wrong way to do art.

Art is...
painting, drawing, pasting, sculpting. It's sewing and building, coloring and folding. It is expressing and observing. Art is getting something that is inside you to the outside.

Part One

Learning About the Elements of Art

Overview of Part One

The activities in Part One introduce the seven basic elements of art. Each section begins with a definition of the element. Each section also provides a series of art experiences that allow young artists to experiment with the element.

The Art Experiences

Experiences are labeled as large-group, small-group, partner, individual, and center activities. Introduce each element with a large-group experience and then extend students' understanding with small-group and independent projects. All of the experiences are designed to encourage students to explore materials and techniques, rather than to simply complete projects.

Contents

How to Use Part One

Preview the Element

Before you begin teaching about an art element, read the definition on the introductory page at the beginning of each section. Think about the element in terms of the following questions:

- Is the element part of your everyday perception?
- How would your world be different without the element?
- Have you ever used the element to express yourself?

Gather the Materials

Use the resource lists to find literature and art that are noted for the use of the art element. Your school library, local museums, online galleries, and art catalogs are important sources to check.

In addition to art reference books you will find in your library, The National Gallery of Art catalog offers a selection of postcards and posters to use as fine art examples. Contact them to receive a copy.

The National Gallery of Art
Mail Order Department
2000 B South Club Drive
Landover, MD 20785

Share Literature and Fine Art Examples

Read several books to your students as part of your daily read-aloud time. Then during your art instruction time, look at the books again. Ask the students to notice the illustrations.

- What things make the illustrations particularly noteworthy?
- How do the illustrations enhance the story?
- Would a different style of illustration change the feeling of the story?

Show fine art examples. Ask students to look thoughtfully at the art and name the things they think contribute to its overall impression. You may want to ask questions such as:

- What is this art showing?
- Is it a happy picture or an unhappy picture?
- What story do you think the artist is trying to tell?
- Does something in the picture make it seem real?

Share the Definition of the Art Element

Hopefully your students will have pointed out the art element during the previous discussions. Use their language and refer to their observations as you present the definition of the art element. After giving the definition, look at the literature illustrations and art examples again, specifically searching for use of the element.

Choose Appropriate Experiences

Next, give students the opportunity to experience the art element in their own lives by doing several of the art activities suggested. Consider your classroom situation and your students when choosing the experiences that you will present. Choose experiences that you and your students will enjoy doing.

Describe the Experiences

Describe the step-by-step procedures for completing an activity, but do not make samples and expect student work to look like the sample. This is a time to encourage creativity.

Display the Student Art

Displaying student art validates the efforts and creativity of your students. As the class views the display, talk again about the art element and the evidence of its use in the completed projects.

Words You Need To Know

Complementary Colors – colors that are straight across from each other on the color wheel

Contrast – using light colors next to dark colors

Cool Colors – colors that have cool undertones: green, blue, and purple

Diagonal – a slanted line

Form – a three-dimensional object

Geometric Shape – a shape that fits into mathematics (circle, square, rectangle, triangle, etc.)

Horizon Line – a horizontal line used to represent the horizon in a one-point perspective drawing

Horizontal – a straight line that runs side to side

Hue – the colors of the color wheel

Line – a basic element of art; the path made by a moving point

Monochromatic – using one color in an image

Organic Shape – a shape that comes from nature and does not fit into mathematics

Parallel Lines – two lines that run next to each other and never intersect

Primary Colors – colors that cannot be made by mixing other colors: red, yellow, and blue

Secondary Colors – colors that are made by mixing two primary colors: orange, green, and purple

Shade – a variety of a particular color with black added

Shape – a basic element of art; an area that is made by a line that touches at the beginning and end

Tertiary Colors – colors that are made by mixing one primary and one secondary color. These colors tend to be grayish. The primary color is always listed first: red-orange, yellow-orange, yellow-green, blue-green, blue-violet, red-violet.

Tint – a variety of a particular color with white added

Value – the use of lights and darks in artwork

Vanishing Point – the single point at which all images vanish in a one-point perspective drawing

Vertical – a straight up and down line

Warm Colors – colors that have warm undertones: red, orange, and yellow

LINE

Learning About
LINE

Lines have names that describe their place in space. They may be diagonal, vertical, or horizontal. Lines may be thick or thin, solid or broken. When two lines sit next to each other they become parallel lines. Lines can be bent into curves and broken into angles.

Lines of All Kinds

Lines have names that describe their place in space. They may be diagonal, vertical, or horizontal. Lines may be thick or thin, solid or broken. When two lines are the same distance apart for their entire length, they are parallel.

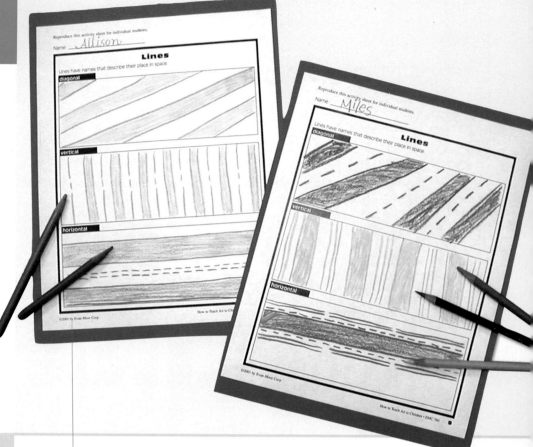

Materials

- crayons or pencils
- sheet on page 9, reproduced for individual students

Step by Step

1. Ask students to look around and name examples of lines that they observe.

2. Introduce the words *diagonal*, *vertical*, and *horizontal* as ways of describing lines in space. Classify classroom examples of each type.

3. Have students draw one line of each type in the appropriate area on the sheet.

4. Have students return to each box and draw another line parallel to each of the original lines.

5. Ask students to shade in the area between the two parallel lines. They will have created a thick line out of two thin lines.

6. Have students add broken lines in each area.

7. Students complete their designs by adding more lines and color.

Reproduce this sheet for individual students to use with Lines of All Kinds on page 8.

Name ___________________________

Lines

Lines have names that describe their place in space.

diagonal

vertical

horizontal

Line Designs

Students plan a design to reinforce their understanding of vertical, horizontal, and diagonal lines.

Materials

(for each group)

• white shelf paper—1 yard (91.5 cm)

• assorted color construction paper strips—1/2" x 12" (1.5 x 30.5 cm)

• felt-tip pens

• glue

• scissors

Step by Step

1. Divide the class into groups of two to four students.

2. Have groups divide their papers into three areas using black pen. Areas may be any configuration the group prefers: squares, overlapping shapes, or equal parts.

3. Students add cut-paper lines to each area. The lines may be thick, thin, solid, or broken.

   • One area should contain only horizontal lines.

   • One area should contain only vertical lines.

   • One area should contain only diagonal lines.

4. Students may choose to add felt-tip lines to enrich the designs.

Curves and Angles

Lines can be bent into curves and broken into angles. In this way, lines can create an infinite number of configurations.

Step by Step

1. Discuss the different types of lines that can be created by changing a straight line into one that bends or curves.

   zigzag

   wavy

   looped

   curly

   scalloped

2. Have students fold their papers into eight equal rectangles.

3. Invite them to create a different type of line in each box.

Materials

• white construction paper—9" x 12" (23 x 30.5 cm)

• crayons

Curved or Bent?

Students combine curved lines and straight lines to create interesting designs.

Materials

- white construction paper—two 6" (15 cm) squares per student
- large piece of black poster paper
- crayons or felt-tip pens

Step by Step

1. Give each student two squares of white construction paper.

2. On one of the squares students will use only straight, bent, and angular lines to create a design.

3. On the other square students will use only curved lines to create a design.

4. When students have finished their designs, group the designs together for display on the black paper.

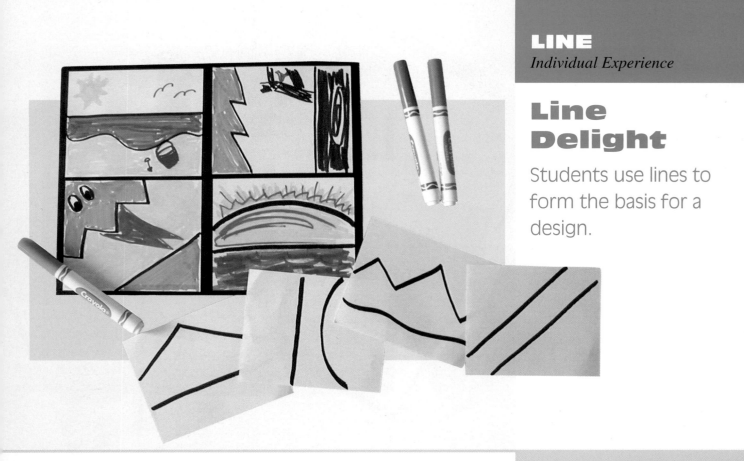

Line Delight

Students use lines to form the basis for a design.

Step by Step

1. Challenge students to create a design beginning with two lines.

   • The lines drawn with black felt-tip pen may be horizontal, vertical, or diagonal.

   • Both lines must travel in the same direction.

   • The lines do not need to be parallel. One line may be curved and the other bent.

2. Students should make three or more different designs in answer to the challenge.

3. Students add color to their designs.

4. Students mount their samples to the black construction paper.

Materials
(for each student)

• white construction paper—four 4" x 5" (10 x 13 cm)

• black construction paper—9" x 12" (23 x 30.5 cm)

• permanent black felt-tip pen or crayon

• markers

Create a Maze

Students tear three blobs from a rectangle and outline the blobs with a continuous line to fill the rectangle.

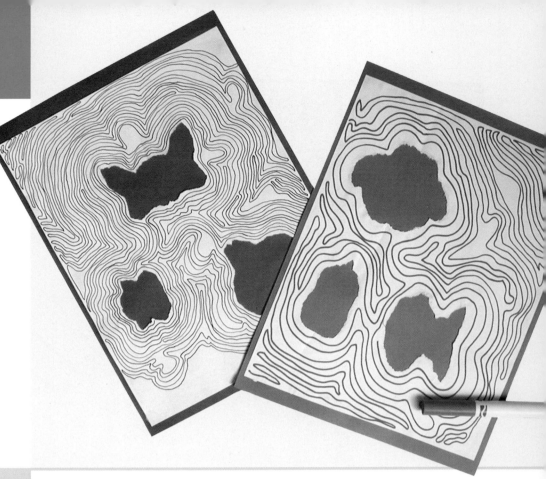

Materials

- white paper—8 1/2" x 11" (21.5 x 28 cm)
- bright-colored paper—9" x 12" (23 x 30.5 cm)
- fine-tip marking pen
- glue

Step by Step

1. Students fold small sections of the paper and tear out three interesting shapes. (Younger students may choose to glue irregular shapes to the white paper instead of tearing out pieces.)

2. The objective is to draw one continuous line. You cannot cross over a line, but you may make a U-turn and go backwards.
   - Using a fine-tip marking pen, begin circling one of the shapes (holes). Before that line comes to a completion, draw toward the next shape.
   - Circle around the second shape, then draw toward the third shape. Continue the line until you have filled the paper.

3. Mount the maze on the bright-colored paper.

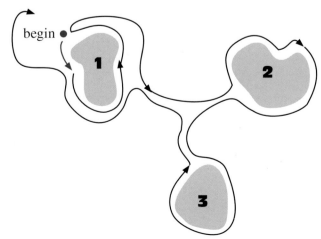

Curved-Line Bookmark

Students cut narrow strips of construction paper in a curve and layer the strips to create a bookmark.

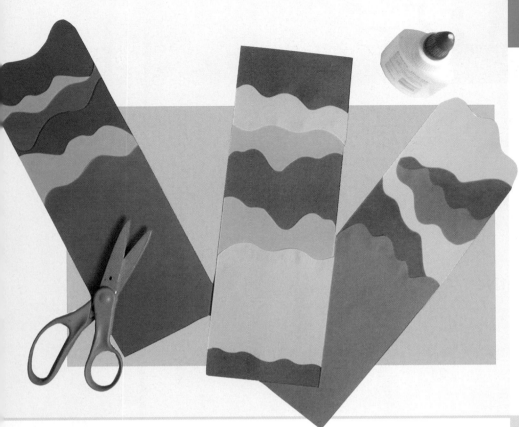

Step by Step

1. Students choose three different colored strips.

2. Students cut each strip into two pieces with a curved cut.

3. Students layer the pieces to create a bookmark. The straight end should always be placed toward the bottom of the bookmark.

4. Glue the pieces together.

5. Laminate for a more lasting bookmark.

Materials

• 3" x 6" (7.5 x 15 cm) colored construction paper strips

• scissors

• glue

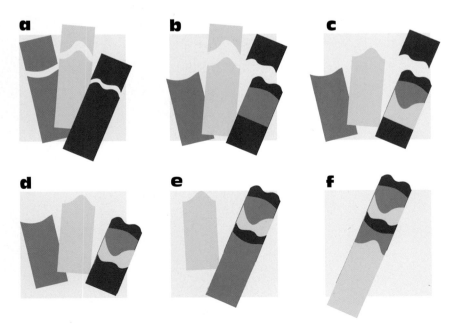

SHAPE

Learning About

SHAPE

Lines create the outline of shapes. Each time a line outlines a shape, it is really creating two images: the positive one and a negative one.

Lines Outline Shapes

Students create the outline of shapes using lines.

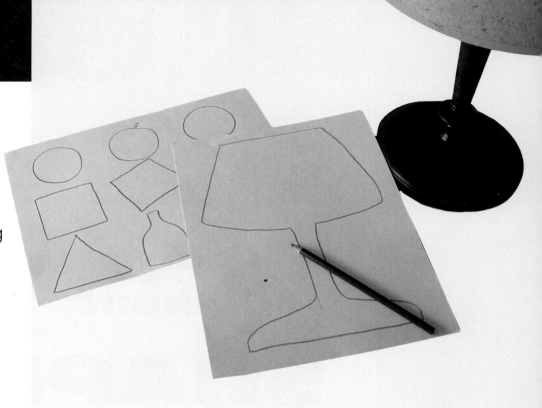

Materials

- newsprint
- pencils

Step by Step

1. Give students pieces of newsprint and invite them to sketch along with you.

2. Draw a circle, a square, and a triangle. Point out that each of these shapes is made up of curved and bent lines. Each is a familiar basic shape that is created by connecting lines.

3. Look at simple objects such as an apple, a bottle, or a vase. Draw an outline of the shapes. (This form of drawing is called contour or outline drawing.)

   - Only the outline of the object is drawn.
   - No inside details are added.

Note: Keep the pencil on the paper while drawing. The resulting drawing may be distorted and exaggerated, but it emphasizes that form is an outline in space that can be manipulated as it is drawn.

A Shape Design

Students create a design using felt shapes and then copy the design onto paper.

Step by Step

1. Students manipulate the felt shapes to create abstract designs on the flannel board. They should experiment with many different designs to see which ones they like the best.

2. Students re-create the designs they developed by drawing and coloring them on a piece of paper.

Materials

- a flannel board
- felt shapes, 3 sizes each:
  circles—red, blue, and yellow
  squares—red, blue, and yellow
  triangles—red, blue, and yellow
  rectangles—red, blue, and yellow
- drawing paper
- red, blue, and yellow crayons

Hint

Try the same experience with wooden blocks or flat plastic shapes.

Positive and Negative Shapes

Every time a line outlines a shape, it is really creating two images: the positive one that is outlined and the negative one that is the background.

Materials

- construction paper in strong, contrasting colors— 6" (15 cm) squares
- glue
- scissors

Step by Step

1. Give each student one square of paper.

2. Students fold the square in half once and cut a shape out of the center. They now have a positive and a negative representation of a shape.

3. Students choose squares of a contrasting color and mount the positive and negative shapes to the contrasting squares.

4. Post the squares around the edge of a bulletin board, window, or chalkboard. Enjoy the shapes!

Shape Designs

Students draw patterns inside a positive shape to create a large, bold design.

Step by Step

1. Students draw large shapes on the white construction paper. The shapes may be circles, squares, triangles, or more complicated contour drawings. It may be easier to fold the paper in half to cut out a symmetrical shape.

2. Students cut out the shapes.

3. Students create a pattern inside the shape.

   • Divide the shape into several parts.

   • Fill each part with a different design or pattern.

4. Mount the shapes on colored pieces of construction paper.

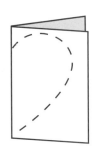

Materials

• white construction paper—
  12" x 18" (30.5 x 46 cm)

• assorted colors of construction paper—12" x 18" (30.5 x 46 cm)

• glue

• scissors

• crayons or felt-tip pens

Shape Search

Some shapes, particularly those used in mathematics, fit definitions and can be given a name. Some shapes are irregular and don't fit a definition. Circles, ovals, crescents, squares, rectangles, triangles, and trapezoids are named shapes. A paint spill might be an irregular shape that doesn't fit a definition.

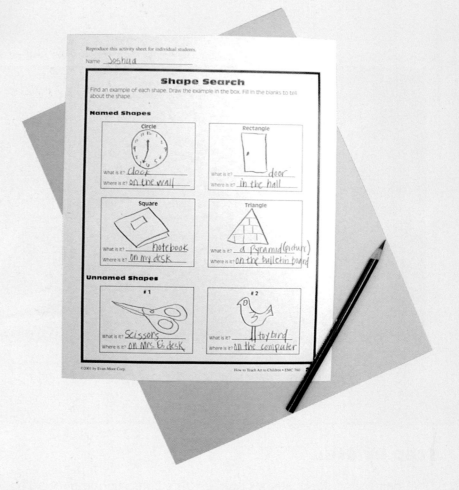

Materials

- sheet on page 23, reproduced for individual students
- crayons or pencils

Step by Step

1. Divide the class into small groups.

2. Give each student a Shape Search sheet.

3. Students in the groups work together to find and name shapes. They should draw examples of the shapes or take photos with a digital camera to document the shapes that they find.

4. Share results of the shape searches with the class.

Reproduce this sheet for individual students to use with Shape Search on page 22.

Name _____

Shape Search

Find an example of each shape. Draw the example in the box. Fill in the blanks to tell about the shape.

Named Shapes

Circle

What is it? _____

Where is it? _____

Rectangle

What is it? _____

Where is it? _____

Square

What is it? _____

Where is it? _____

Triangle

What is it? _____

Where is it? _____

Unnamed Shapes

#1

What is it? _____

Where is it? _____

#2

What is it? _____

Where is it? _____

What Is It?

Each student uses the same shape and creates a picture incorporating the shape. Pictures are compared to document the variety.

Materials

- construction paper—
  blue 2" (5 cm) circles
  white 6" (15 cm) squares

- glue

- crayons

Step by Step

1. Students glue one blue circle on one white square.

2. Students draw lines to complete a picture. The blue circle must be a part of the picture.

3. Compare the completed pictures. Discuss the different things the blue circles represent.

Hint

Extend this project by using different shapes and colors in the project. Older students may enjoy the challenge of using several shapes at the same time.

A Shape Collage

Students cut two identical shapes into pieces. Then they put the pieces back together and create a collage.

Step by Step

1. Students choose two scraps of wrapping paper that are about the same size.

   • Students hold the two pieces together as they cut out a circle, triangle, or square.

   • Holding the two identical shapes together, the students fold the shape in half.

   • Cut out the center of the shape.

   • Additional cuts are made to the remaining shape.

2. Students glue the pieces on the construction paper square using parts of one colored shape to complete the other colored shape.

Materials

• 9" (23 cm) square of construction paper

• scraps of wrapping paper

• scissors

• glue

a   b   c   d

COLOR

Learning About

COLOR

Color is a sensation produced by various rays
of light of different wavelengths.

Primary Colors

There are three primary colors: red, yellow, and blue. These colors are called primary colors because you can mix them to create all the colors of the rainbow. The colors create the foundation of the color wheel.

Materials

- miscellaneous objects in the three primary colors
- colorful classroom

Step by Step

1. Display the three primary colors. Brainstorm things often associated with each color.

   > yellow—sun, lemons, flowers, school buses
   > blue—sky, water, jeans
   > red—apples, fire, roses, sunsets, hearts

2. Discuss how each color has certain feelings associated with it.

   > yellow—cheerful
   > blue—cool or sad
   > red—angry or hot

3. Invite students to look around the room and identify red objects. Ask, "Does red look the same each time?"

4. Take a red sweater and compare how light or dark the red seems to be depending on whether it is located in a dark closet or out in the sunlight. Help students conclude that any color may be altered by the amount of light that surrounds it.

A Primary Color Quilt Design

Students create paper quilts using primary-colored squares.

Step by Step

1. Divide the class into groups of two to four students.

2. Students meet in their groups gathered around the butcher paper grid. They place the larger primary-colored paper squares on the butcher paper.

   Note: Experimenting with different arrangements should be encouraged. There is no "correct" way to arrange the colors; it is entirely up to group tastes.

3. Next the students place the smaller paper squares on top of the large squares. Many combinations may be tried before the students decide on the final arrangement.

4. Students glue all squares in place.

5. Display all group designs when they are finished.

Materials
(for each group)

- construction paper—

   9" (23 cm) squares:
   three blue
   three red
   three yellow

   3" (7.5 cm) squares:
   three blue
   three red
   three yellow

- butcher paper—
   27" (69 cm) square folded into
   9" (23 cm) squares

- glue

One-Color Art

Students create simple drawings with one primary color.

Materials
(for each student)

- construction paper—three white 12" (30.5 cm) squares
- red, yellow, and blue crayons
- black crayon or felt-tip pen (optional)

Step by Step

1. Challenge students to draw three objects or pictures. They should use only one primary color for each picture. (Black may be used to outline or add details to each of the pictures.)

2. When students have completed their work, display the same color pictures together.

3. Discuss the display.
   - Were the subjects of one color similar?
   - Do students have a different feeling looking at the pictures of different colors?

Three-Color Paint Job

Students paint pictures using the three primary colors.

Step by Step

1. Reproduce the painting challenges below and prepare the center.

2. Students go to the art center, choose a challenge, and use the three colors provided to paint.

3. Discuss the effect of using the three primary colors together.

Painting Challenges

- Paint a beach ball rolling into the sea.
- Paint a rowboat on the lake on a sunny day.
- Paint red, blue, and yellow fruit.
- Paint an airplane zooming over a circus tent.
- Paint a watering can in a flower garden.
- Paint a child with an umbrella walking in the rain.
- Paint the wind vane on the top of a barn.
- Paint a child with a wagon.

Materials

- large white painting paper
- red, yellow, and blue tempera paint
- brushes in a variety of sizes
- painting challenges written on note cards

Design a Flag

Students create flags using the three primary colors.

Materials

(for each student)

• construction paper—

  white 9" x 12" (23 x 30.5 cm)

  red 6" (15 cm) square

  blue 6" (15 cm) square

  yellow 6" (15 cm) square

• glue

• scissors

• black crayon (optional)

Step by Step

1. Students plan and design flags using the three primary colors. They may cut the three primary-colored squares into any shape.

2. Encourage them to experiment and try several different designs before gluing the pieces in place.

3. Students may add details with the black crayon.

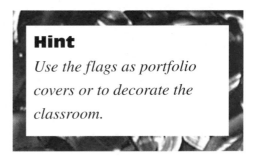

Hint

Use the flags as portfolio covers or to decorate the classroom.

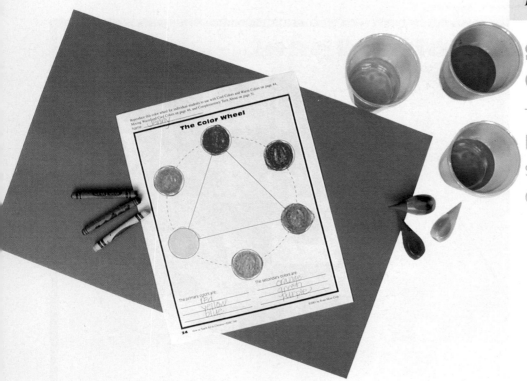

Secondary Colors

The primary colors can be mixed to create the secondary colors of orange, green, and violet.

Step by Step

1. Place the three small jars of primary colors on the overhead projector in the positions shown on the color wheel sheet. Add three empty jars in the positions of the secondary colors.

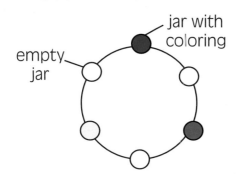

empty jar

jar with coloring

2. Use an eyedropper to mix the primary colors, creating secondary colors in the empty jars. Stir to mix. Always begin with the lightest color and add the darker color one drop at a time.

3. When all the mixing is complete, you will have created the three secondary colors—purple, orange, and green.

4. Have students use colored pencils or crayons and the color wheel sheet to show how the secondary colors are made.

Note: In this book the word purple is used instead of violet as it is the word commonly used on classroom crayons, construction paper, and paint.

Materials

- food coloring and water premixed in glass jars for the three primary colors—red, blue, and yellow

- small glass bowls or plastic glasses

- three eyedroppers

- overhead projector

- color wheel sheet on page 34, reproduced for individual students

- colored pencils or crayons

Reproduce this color wheel for individual students to use with Secondary Colors on page 33, Cool Colors and Warm Colors on page 44, Mixing Warm and Cool Colors on page 46, and Complementary Turn About on page 51.

Name _____

The Color Wheel

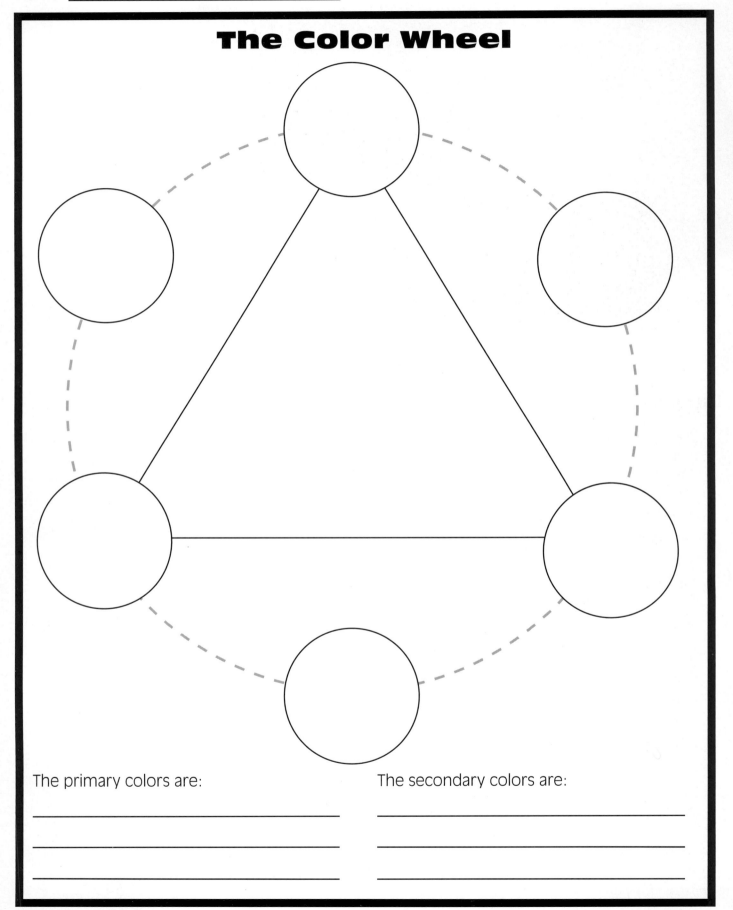

The primary colors are:

_____

_____

_____

The secondary colors are:

_____

_____

_____

Color Memory Game

This activity reinforces color memory and expands students' color awareness.

Step by Step

1. Write numbers on each matching construction paper pair—strip and square.

2. Put the strips in the container. Lay the squares, numbers facing down, in random order on a table.

3. Put a chair in front of the table but facing away from the table.

4. One student sits in the chair and picks a colored strip from the can. The student reads the number aloud and studies the color for a few seconds before replacing the strip.

5. The student turns around and finds the matching color square on the table. The student reads the number to verify that it is the correct match.

Materials
(for each group)

- construction paper—several shades of every color

  2" (5 cm) strips

  4" (10 cm) squares, matching colors

- can or plastic container

Hint

This game becomes even more challenging if duplicate paint chips from the paint store are used in place of construction paper strips and squares.

Color Mixing for All

Each student can experience the magic of color mixing in the art center.

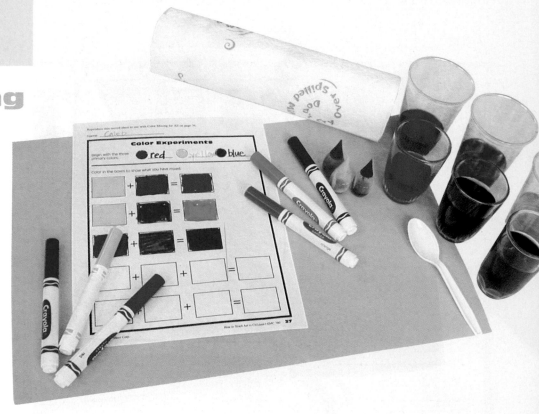

Materials

- a pitcher of water
- six clear plastic drinking glasses
- a spoon
- small squeeze-type bottles of red, blue, and yellow food coloring
- Color Experiments sheet on page 37, reproduced for individual students
- paper towels
- a plastic tub or sink for cleanup
- markers

Step by Step

1. Set up the color mixing center.

2. Students visit the center and experiment with mixing the primary colors. Remind students to always begin with the lightest color and add the darker color one drop at a time.

3. Using markers, students record the colors mixed on the sheet.

4. Challenge students to mix three colors and discover new shades.

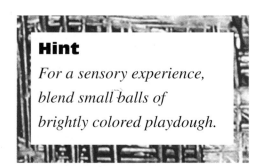

Hint

For a sensory experience, blend small balls of brightly colored playdough.

Name _____

Color Experiments

Begin with the three primary colors.

Color in the boxes to show what you have mixed.

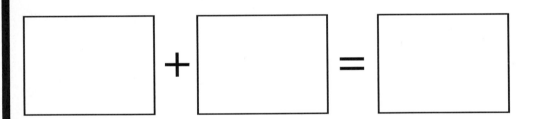

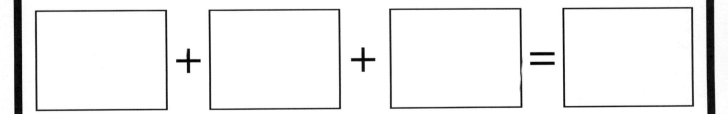

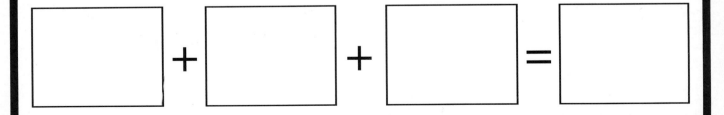

Mixing Gradations of Color

Students discover that mixing different amounts of a color changes the color's hue.

Materials

- tempera or watercolor paint
- brushes
- plate or foam tray for mixing colors
- water and paper towels
- Changing Colors sheet on page 39, reproduced for individual students

Step by Step

1. A student paints the first square on the sheet and makes a dab of the same color on the plate.

2. The student follows the directions on the sheet to add more color. After mixing a new color on the plate, the student paints the square below.

3. The student continues to mix and paint to fill in each square on the sheet.

4. Let the sheets dry completely.

Hint

Students may enjoy creating a design picture using the colored squares from the sheet. The squares may be cut out and arranged in interesting designs on another sheet of paper.

Name _____

Changing Colors

Mix the paint colors to create new hues.

YELLOW	RED	YELLOW
Add red	Add blue	Add blue
Add more red	Add more blue	Add more blue
Add more red	Add more blue	Add more blue

The Background Makes a Difference

Contrast is the degree of difference between colors or tones in a piece of artwork.

Materials

- a basket of small colorful objects
- colored construction paper— 12" x 18" (30.5 x 46 cm) sheets

Step by Step

1. Students choose an item and lay it on a colored background.

2. Students change the background to see if one color presents the item in a better way. Which combinations of color have the best contrast?

3. Students explain which color is their favorite and why they chose it.

Hint

Create an interesting bulletin board. Use squares of different-colored construction paper as the background. Mount the same object on all the squares.

Pick Contrasting Colors

Students manipulate colors to discover which colors make good contrasts.

Step by Step

1. Students begin by laying out all six of the larger squares.

2. Then they place one of the smaller squares in the center of each larger one.

3. They keep rearranging the smaller squares until they find the three best contrasting combinations.

4. They use their crayons to record those combinations on their sheets.

5. Next, the students decide which three combinations of colors represent samples of least contrast. Students move the colored squares and record their choices on the sheets.

6. Finally, students record their favorite combinations.

7. Have students share their results. Did the students all choose the same combinations? Are there combinations of colors that are not contrasting but are still pleasing to the students?

Materials
(for each student)

• construction paper—

 six 5" (13 cm) squares of red, orange, yellow, green, blue, purple

 six 2" (5 cm) squares in the same colors

• Contrasting Colors sheet on page 42, reproduced for individual students

• crayons

Name _____

Contrasting Colors

Best Contrast: ▬▬▬▬▬▬▬▬▬▬▬▬▬▬▬▬▬▬▬▬▬▬▬▬

Least Contrast: ▬▬▬▬▬▬▬▬▬▬▬▬▬▬▬▬▬▬▬▬▬▬▬

Favorite Combinations: ▬▬▬▬▬▬▬▬▬▬▬▬▬▬▬▬▬▬

Contrasting Backgrounds

Students experience how contrasting colors affect their artwork. They will choose a background that creates the effect they desire.

Step by Step

1. Students draw a shape on each of their smaller squares.

2. Students cut out the shapes.

3. Students experiment with background color by laying their cut out shapes on several different colors of background paper.

4. Students choose the colors they like best and glue on the shape.

> yellow on yellow = poor contrast
>
> yellow on purple = strong contrast
>
> yellow on red = good contrast, warm colors

Materials
(for each student)

- colored construction paper— assortment of 6" (15 cm) and 3" (7.5 cm) squares

- pencil

- scissors

- glue

Cool Colors and Warm Colors

Blue, green, and purple are often labeled as cool colors. Yellow, orange, and red are called warm colors. Students categorize colors as cool and warm.

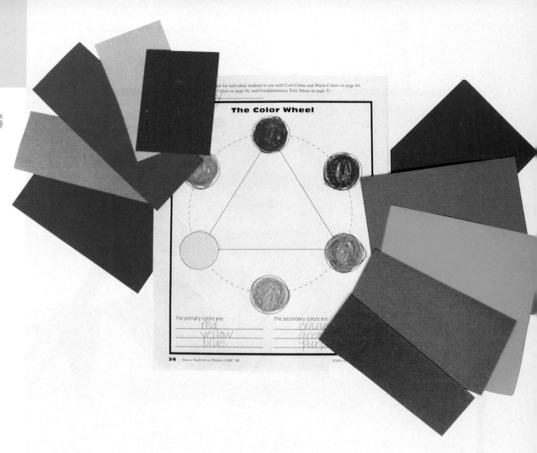

Materials

- *Owl Moon* by Jane Yolen; Philomel
- *Arrow to the Sun* by Gerald McDermott; Viking Press
- colored paper scraps
- color wheel

Step by Step

1. Read the book *Owl Moon*. Discuss the illustrator's choice of colors to depict the moonlit winter night.

2. Read *Arrow to the Sun*. Discuss the illustrator's choice of colors.

3. Compare the colors used in the two books and the two different settings.

4. Sort the colored paper scraps into two piles:
   - colors that fit the cool winter setting of *Owl Moon*
   - colors that fit the warm desert setting of *Arrow to the Sun*

5. Look at the color wheel and notice how it has been divided into cool colors and warm colors as well.

all warm · mostly cool · mostly warm · all cool

Colorful Collage

Students work with warm and cool colors to develop a collage.

Step by Step

1. Divide the class into small groups.

2. Have each group fold their butcher paper square into fourths. Label the sections of the paper: all warm, all cool, mostly warm (with a cool accent), mostly cool (with a warm accent).

3. Each group searches through the magazines to find patches of color that fit one of the categories. Samples may be torn or cut from the magazines and glued in the correct section.

4. When all the groups have finished, it is interesting to compare the final effects. The group papers may be cut into separate sections and framed as a display in the classroom.

Materials
(for each group)

- magazines
- white butcher paper—36" (91.5 cm) square
- scissors
- glue

Hint

Photographs with lots of white will not be as effective as solid-color photographs.

Mixing Warm and Cool Colors

Students experiment with color to create variations of the basic color wheel hues.

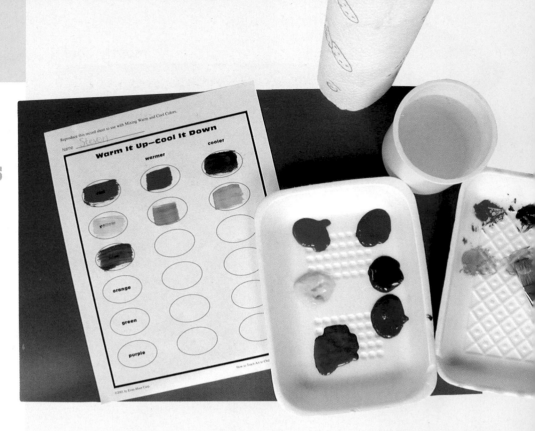

Materials

(for each student)

- tempera paint—
  red, yellow, blue, orange, green, purple
- brush
- water
- plates or foam trays for mixing colors
- Warm It Up—Cool It Down sheet on page 47

Step by Step

1. Students begin with red. They paint the spot on the sheet with red paint.

2. Students add a warm primary color to red to make a warmer red and paint the warm red spot on the sheet.

3. Students add a cool primary color to red to make a cooler red and paint the cool red spot on the sheet.

4. Students continue experimenting with each color on the color wheel.

Hint

Keep pure primary colors on one plate or tray. Mix colors on a second tray.

Name _____

Warm It Up—Cool It Down

	warmer	cooler
red		
yellow		
blue		
orange		
green		
purple		

My Favorite Palette

After students have experimented with mixing variations of the primary and secondary colors, they choose a color combination that they prefer.

Materials

- paper for painting
- tempera paints
- brushes
- water
- plates for mixing colors

Step by Step

1. Set up a paint center with a job card asking students to select their favorite palette.

2. Students paint a picture using their chosen palette.

3. Students write an explanation of why they chose the palette they did.

4. Display student artwork and written explanations.

Pick a Palette

Paint a picture with the palette you like the best.

   Warm colors only

   Cool colors only

   Warm colors with a cool accent

   Cool colors with a warm accent

Complementary Colors

Complementary colors
are pairs of colors that sit
opposite one another on
the color wheel.

Step by Step

1. Fold the butcher paper into 6" squares and then open it up and press it flat. Pin it to a bulletin board.

2. Give each student a 6" square and a 2" square of the colored construction paper in complementary colors.

3. First, students take turns pinning up the large colored squares onto the butcher paper. They may choose any available position for their squares.

4. Then students take turns pinning their small squares within a large square of a complementary color. Small squares may be positioned anywhere within the larger squares: in the center, in a corner, etc.

Materials

• butcher paper—
  36" (91.5 cm) square

• construction paper—

  6" (15 cm) squares—six each:
  red, orange, yellow, green,
  blue, purple

  2" (5 cm) squares—six each:
  red, orange, yellow, green,
  blue, purple

• straight pins

Complementary Rip and Paste

Students demonstrate that they can identify complementary colors as they create an abstract design.

Materials

(for each student)

- construction paper—

  white 9" x 12" (23 x 30.5 cm)

  4" (10 cm) squares—red, orange, yellow, green, blue, purple

- glue

Step by Step

1. Explain that this project has one rule—only complementary colors may touch each other.

2. Students rip off a piece of each colored square.

3. Remembering the rule, students lay all the pieces on the white construction paper in a random design.

4. Students add additional ripped pieces to create a pleasing design.

5. Glue the pieces in place.

Hint

Laminate the rip-and-paste designs. Use as a cover for a writing log or an assignment book.

Complementary Turn About

This cut-and-paste project results in a striking design. Use it for the cover of a folder or portfolio.

Step by Step

1. Students choose a 12" square and four 6" squares of a complementary color.

2. Students draw an interesting line across one of the 6" squares.

3. Holding the four small squares together, students cut along the line.

4. Students fold the 12" square into quarters and then open it up.

5. Students glue one of the cut pieces in each section of the larger square. The result is a design that is a striking use of complementary colors and a simple repetitive design.

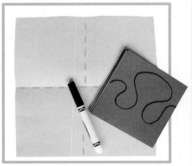 

Materials
(for each student)

- construction paper—

  four 6" (15 cm) squares— Provide a choice of all the colors on the color wheel.

  12" (30.5 cm) square—Provide a choice of all the colors on the color wheel.

- pencil or marker
- glue
- scissors

Tertiary Colors

Tertiary colors are colors created by the mixing of secondary colors. Mixing these hues tends to create colors with a grayish or muted effect.

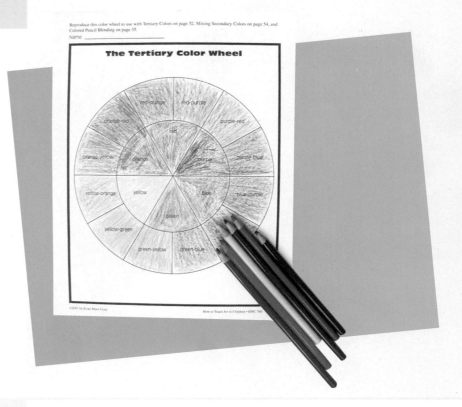

Reproduce this color wheel to use with Tertiary Colors on page 52, Mixing Secondary Colors on page 54, and Colored Pencil Blending on page 55.

Name _____

The Tertiary Color Wheel

red-orange · red-purple · orange-red · purple-red · orange-yellow · orange · red · purple · purple-blue · yellow-orange · yellow · blue · purple-blue · green · blue-purple · yellow-green · green-yellow · green-blue

©2001 by Evan-Moor Corp.   How to Teach Art to Children • EMC 760

Materials
(for each student)

- Tertiary Color Wheel on page 53, reproduced for individual students
- colored pencils or crayons in six colors on the color wheel
- clipboards
- pencils

Step by Step

1. Have students color in the Tertiary Color Wheel sheet. They should blend the colors of the basic color wheel to make the tertiary colors.

2. Take the class on a walk around the playground or neighborhood. Help students identify tertiary colors in their environment. Have each student list two examples by each color.

gray-green

yellow-green

blue-green

Reproduce this color wheel to use with Tertiary Colors on page 52, Mixing to Match on page 54, and Colored Pencil Blending on page 55.

Name _____

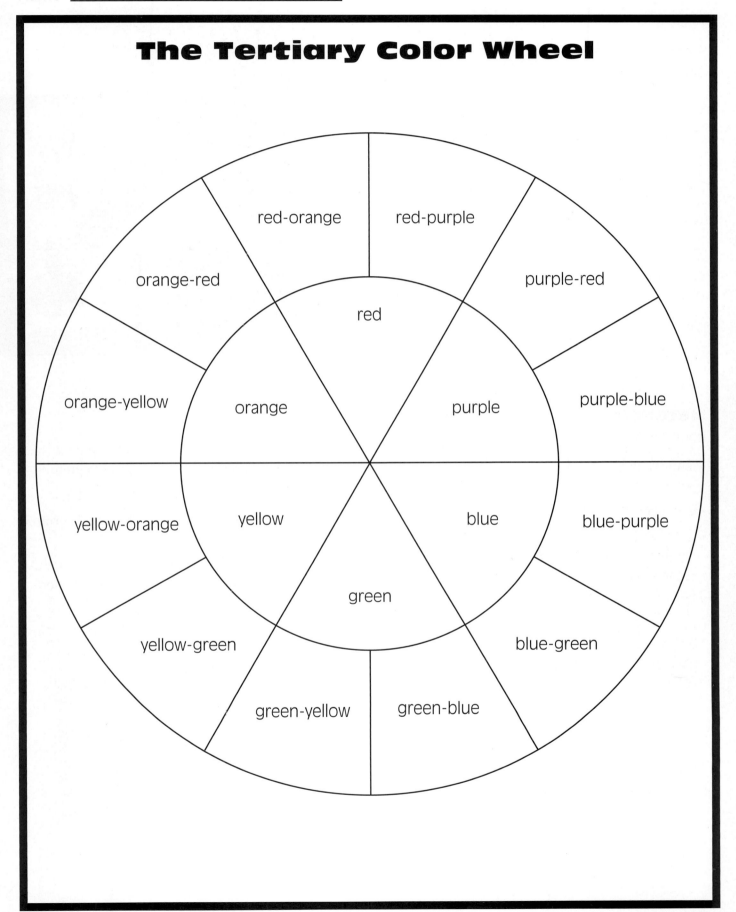

The Tertiary Color Wheel

red-orange

red-purple

orange-red

purple-red

red

orange-yellow

purple-blue

orange

purple

purple-blue

yellow-orange

blue

blue-purple

yellow

green

blue-green

yellow-green

green-yellow

green-blue

Mixing to Match

Students mix secondary colors to match the colors they see in nature.

Materials
(for each group)

- tempera paints—red, orange, yellow, green, blue, purple
- white construction paper
- small items from the classroom and nature that have muted colors—leaves, rocks, flowers, rusted pipes, erasers, wood chips
- glue
- plate or foam tray for mixing colors
- brush
- water
- paper towels
- Tertiary Color Wheel on page 53

Step by Step

1. Divide the class into small groups. Have groups color in their Tertiary Color Wheels if they have not been completed before.

2. Give each group four or five items to use for color matching.

3. Students lay each item beside the colors on the wheel to determine which colors are the closest matches.

4. Students mix the paint until they feel they have reached a good match. They paint a sample splotch on the white paper and then glue the items next to the mixed colors.

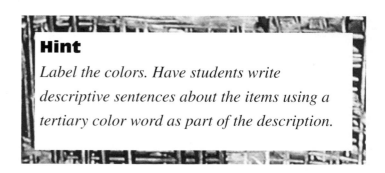

Hint
Label the colors. Have students write descriptive sentences about the items using a tertiary color word as part of the description.

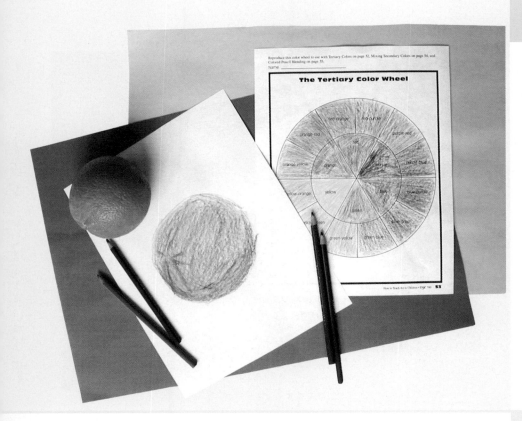

Colored Pencil Blending

Students find out how pencil layering of primary and secondary colors can achieve a muted, tertiary effect.

Step by Step

1. Students practice layering one colored pencil over a different colored pencil. Light and consistent pressure on the pencil will achieve successful layering.

2. Student complete the Tertiary Color Wheel sheet using this layering technique.

3. Students create a picture using the pencils and tertiary color. You may want to provide simple objects as models—pieces of fruit, interesting leaves, small rocks, or potted plants.

Materials
(for each student)

• colored pencils
• The Tertiary Color Wheel on page 53
• white drawing paper

Rainbow of Colors

Students build colorful mosaic pictures with paper scraps cut from magazines.

Materials

- white construction paper
- magazines
- scissors
- glue

Step by Step

1. Have students cut out small squares of colors from magazines.

2. Students begin by dividing the colors into warm-color and cool-color piles. Then they separate those piles into more defined piles of secondary and tertiary colors.

3. Once they have at least six piles (red, orange, yellow, green, blue, violet), have them glue the squares into place to form a design or a block letter that has been traced onto white paper.

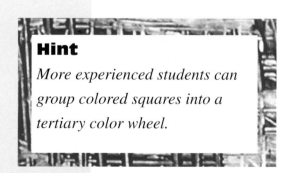

Hint

More experienced students can group colored squares into a tertiary color wheel.

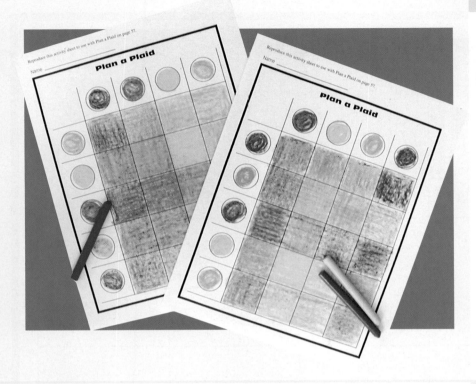

Plan a Plaid

Students create a plaid pattern by filling in a grid.

Step by Step

1. Students begin by choosing a color for each of the four circles across the top of the grid. They color in those circles.

2. Next, they color the five boxes below the first circle the same color that appears in that circle.

3. They move to the next vertical row of boxes and color them to match the circle color at the top of that row. They continue until all of the rows are colored to match each of the circles above.

4. Now they choose a color for each of the five circles down the left side of the grid.

5. They color the first horizontal row of boxes to match the first circle on the left. They have already colored those boxes once to match the top circles, so now they will be lightly placing another color over the top. It begins to lend an interesting plaid effect.

6. They move to the next row and repeat the process until the whole page is finished.

Materials

• Plan a Plaid sheet on page 58, reproduced for individual students

• crayons

Name _____

Plan a Plaid

	◯	◯	◯	◯
◯				
◯				
◯				
◯				
◯				

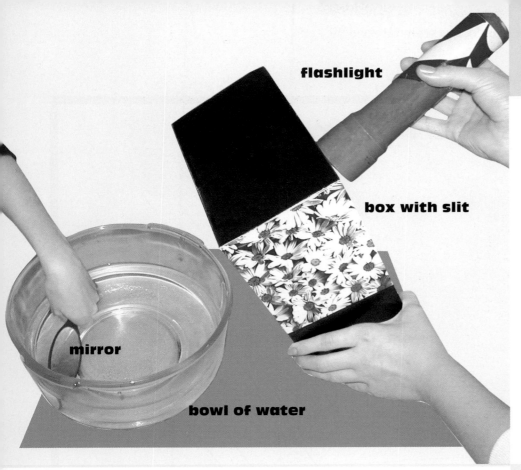

flashlight

box with slit

mirror

bowl of water

The Whole Spectrum

Students have first-hand experience creating their own rainbow of light using water and a mirror.

Step by Step

1. Students assemble equipment as shown in the picture.

2. Students move the mirror to create a spectrum of light on the ceiling.

3. Discuss group results:

   • Were they able to create the spectrum in more than one way?

   • Was the intensity of colors different using different methods?

   • Why does the mirror work as a prism?

   • Are there other ways to create a spectrum of light?

4. Students should fill in the colors they observed on the sheet.

Materials
(for each group)

• tub or bowl of water

• small mirror

• flashlight

• cardboard box with a slit in the bottom

• The Prism sheet on page 60, reproduced for individual students

Note: Intermediate students need to know that light is made up of a band or a spectrum of color. These colors travel in waves and each color has a different wavelength. You can prove this by letting light pass through a three-sided piece of glass called a prism. The light that appears clear is changed into seven colors as it passes through the prism: red, orange, yellow, green, blue, violet, and indigo.

Name _____

The Prism

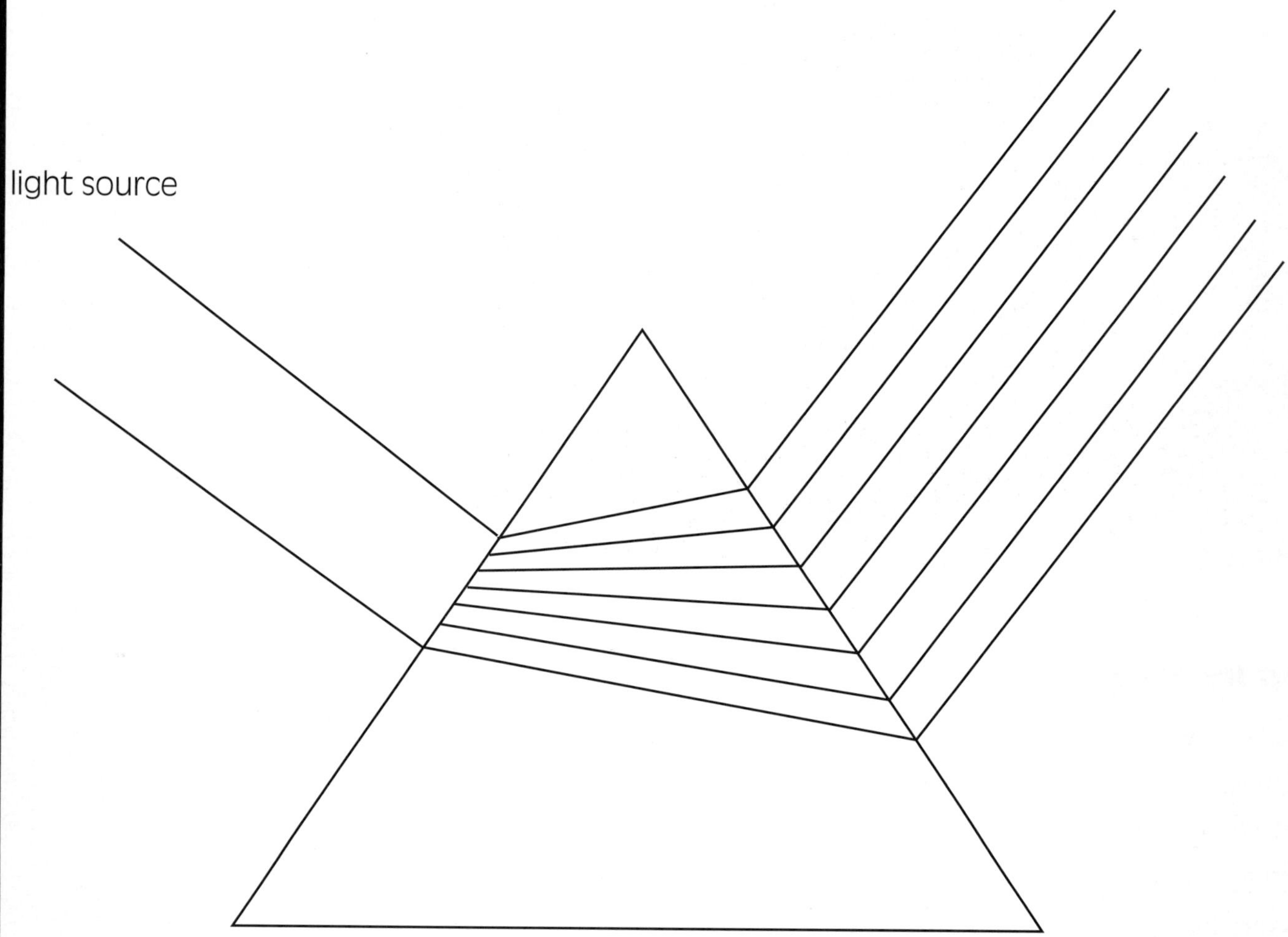

light source

What I Observed

_____

_____

_____

_____

_____

Prism Art

Students use what they have learned about the spectrum of colors to create a design.

Step by Step

1. Students draw a triangle in the center of the construction paper. This triangle represents a prism.

2. Beginning at the top, students draw lines radiating from the triangle. Lines should be drawn in sets of seven similar lines, creating a section for each color in the spectrum.

3. Students color in the design following the order in which the colors appear in the spectrum.

Materials
(for each student)

• white construction paper—
  12" x 18" (30.5 x 46 cm)

• crayons or felt-tip pens

• pencil

Hint

Cut out the designs and mount the cutouts on black paper. Discuss the way the eye is drawn to the center of the shape.

VALUE

Learning About

VALUE

Any hue or color on the color wheel may have an infinite number of values or tones. When colors are used at full value, they appear strong and bright. When colors are mixed with white paint or water, they appear as muted, lighter tones.

Black and White

Black and white offer a striking contrast when used together and create a strong visual image.

Materials
(for each student)

- construction paper—

  black 9" x 12" (23 x 30.5 cm)

  white 9" x 6" (23 x 15 cm)

- scissors
- glue
- pencil

Step by Step

1. Students draw several light pencil lines from the top to the bottom of the white paper.

2. Students cut the white paper on the pencil lines.

3. Students spread out the white strips across the black paper.

4. Students experiment with variations and then glue the white strips in place.

Hint
*Read **Black and White** by David Macaulay. Note the strong visual images that tell the story.*

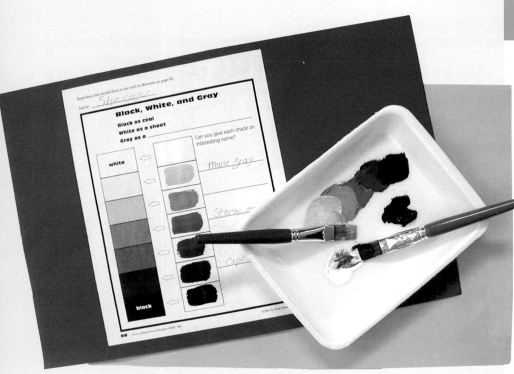

In Between

Tones of gray exist between black and white. This activity involves the creation of a light to dark scale and requires careful mixing of colors.

Step by Step

1. Students begin by painting in the white box on the Black, White, and Gray sheet. Then they paint the black box.

2. Next they mix the middle tone. They begin by putting white on their plates and slowly adding drops of black until they create the gray that they feel should be in the middle.

3. After painting the middle tone, students mix gradations of gray and fill in the other four boxes.

4. Challenge students to give each in-between color a new name.

Materials
(for each student)

- tempera paint—white and black
- paintbrush
- water for cleaning the brush
- paper towels
- plate or foam tray for mixing colors
- Black, White, and Gray sheet on page 66

Name _____

Black, White, and Gray

Black as coal

White as a sheet

Gray as a _____

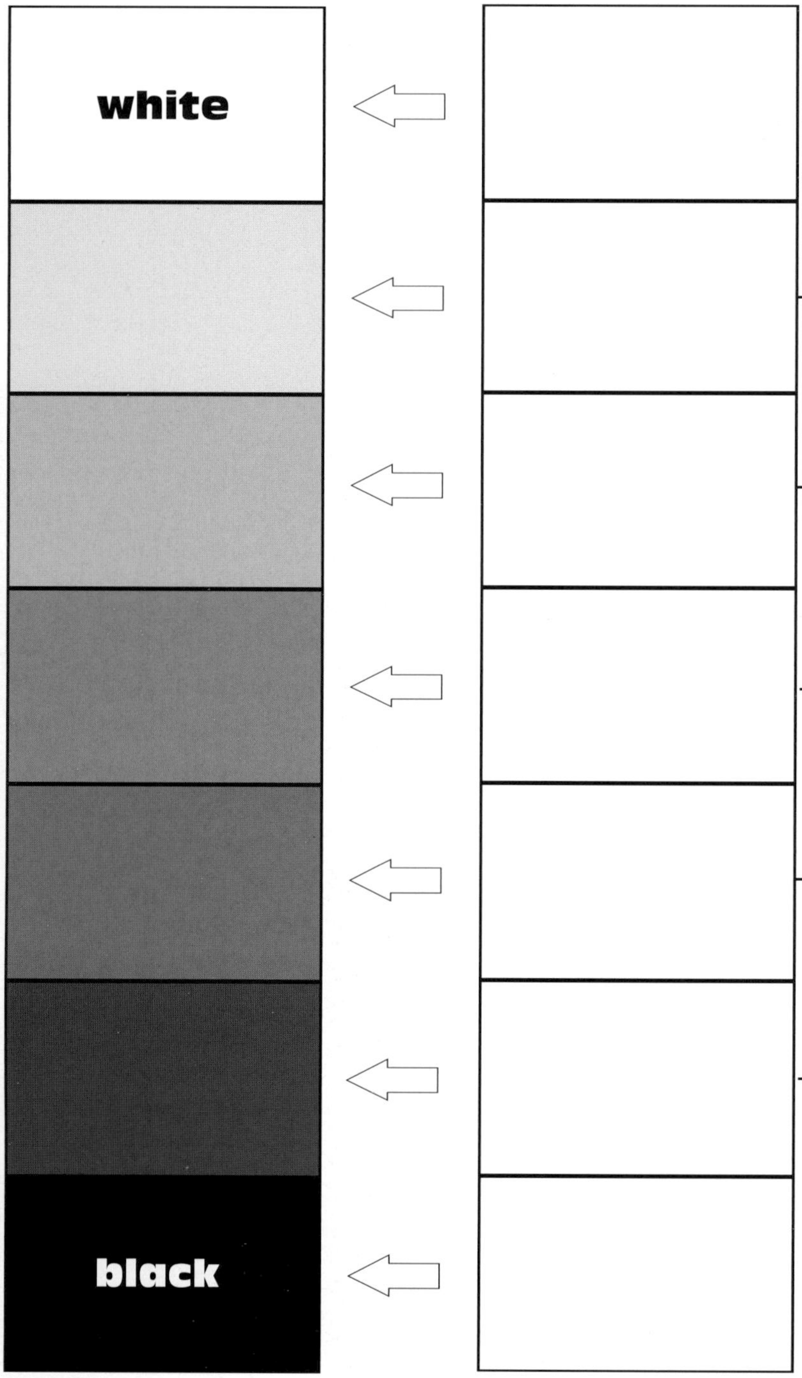

white		

Can you give each shade an interesting name?

black

A cat on a foggy day.

Paint an airplane in a cloud.

Grays All Around

Students experiment with black, white, and gray paint.

Step by Step

1. Challenge students to think of an object or scene that could be gray.

2. Students mix black and white to make various shades of gray.

3. Students complete their pictures using only black, white, and gray.

Materials

- tempera paint—black and white
- plate for mixing paint
- paintbrush
- white easel paper

Painting Challenges

- Snowman in a Snowstorm
- Cat on a Foggy Day
- Cityscape at Night
- Train in a Tunnel
- Airplane in a Cloud

Colors Have Many Values

Students experiment with the values of colors.

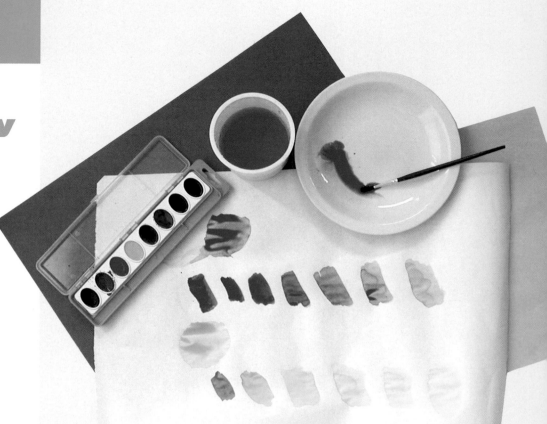

Materials
(for each student)

- tray of watercolor paints
- large watercolor brush
- butcher paper
- plate or dish
- cup of water

Step by Step

1. Students create a colored puddle on their mixing plate using a full-strength primary color. Now paint a blotch of that same color on the white paper.

2. Adding a brushful of water to the colored puddle on the plate, students create a muted value of the first shade. Now paint a sample of that value on the white paper.

3. Students keep adding water and making blotches until the color ranges from a strong, pure value to a muted, pale value.

4. Students repeat the steps, using a different color.

Hint
Have students compare the color to an emotion. A strong emotion like **anger** *can be diluted to a muted emotion like* **irritation***.*

Light and Dark

Students demonstrate that any color can have more than one value.

Step by Step

1. Divide the class into pairs. Give each pair one piece of paper and 8 different crayons.

2. Demonstrate how to fold the construction paper into 16 squares.

3. One student in the pair picks a color and colors any one of the boxes on the paper with a firm, solid stroke. The partner then uses that same color but shades in another box with a pale version of the original color.

4. The partners continue coloring with all 8 crayons, one dark box and one pale box.

5. Create a frame for the design by gluing it to a colored construction paper square.

6. Display all of the finished squares on a bulletin board.

Materials
(for each pair of students)

- construction paper—
  white 11" (28 cm) square
  colored 12" (30.5 cm) square
- box of crayons
- glue

Mixing Colors with White

Colors mixed with white are called tints. This project encourages students to create tints of the color wheel colors.

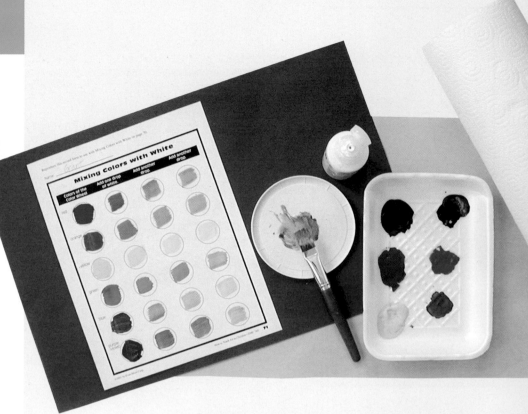

Materials

- a set of tempera colors—red, orange, yellow, green, blue, purple, white
- paintbrush
- plate or foam tray
- access to a sink or washing station
- paper towels
- Mixing Colors with White sheet on page 71, reproduced for individual students

Step by Step

1. Students begin with a small puddle of red paint on the plate. They paint the circle marked "red" on the sheet.

2. Students add one drop of white paint to the red puddle. They mix this new color and paint the next circle on the sheet.

3. Students add another drop of white paint to the same puddle of color and paint the next circle with this lighter tone.

4. Students add one more drop of white to the same puddle and paint the next circle.

5. This procedure should be followed for the other colors on the color wheel. The plate and brush should be rinsed before working with a new color.

Reproduce this sheet to use with Mixing Colors with White on page 70.

Name _____

Mixing Colors with White

Colors of the Color Wheel	Add one drop of white.	Add another drop.	Add another drop.
red			
orange			
yellow			
green			
blue			
purple (violet)			

Shading Shapes

Students discover that shading adds dimension to shapes.

Materials
(for each student)

• newsprint

• pencils

Step by Step

Direct students to complete the two drawings below:

Drawing 1

1. Draw a ball.

2. Pretend the sun is in the top left corner of the page.

3. Shade the right side of the ball.

4. Lay in a shadow on the ground.

Drawing 2

1. Draw a box.

2. Pretend the sun is in the top right corner of the page.

3. Shade the left side of the box.

4. Lay in a shadow on the ground.

5. Make the box into a house.

6. Add shading to the dark side of the house.

7. Draw a ball or a tree in the yard. Which way will the shadow go?

Two Butterflies

Students cut out and paint a butterfly using one color plus white paint.

Step by Step

1. Students fold the white construction paper in half and outline with pencil one-half of a butterfly shape. They cut on that line.

2. Students open the butterfly shape and use their pencil to lightly sketch a line along the outside border. Then they pencil in various shapes in the center of the butterfly.

3. Now students use their acrylic paints to paint their butterfly using only one color of paint mixed with white to create different values of that color.

   • First they paint the outside border with the solid color. It will have the darkest value.

   • Then they mix that color with a little white and paint some of the shapes in the center of the butterfly.

   • They continue adding white to the previous color and painting until they have a very muted shade of the original color.

4. Allow the butterflies to dry. Display all students' work so they can appreciate the interesting effects created by using just one color plus white in a design.

Materials
(for each student)

• white construction paper— 12" x 18" (30.5 x 46 cm)

• acrylic paints in various colors, including white

• brushes in several sizes

• paper plate for mixing paint

• pencil

TEXTURE

Learning About

TEXTURE

The world is full of a variety of textures. Students have first-hand experiences with many textures. They know about rough rocks and smooth marbles.

Awareness of Texture

Students investigate their world and describe what they see and touch in terms of how it looks and feels.

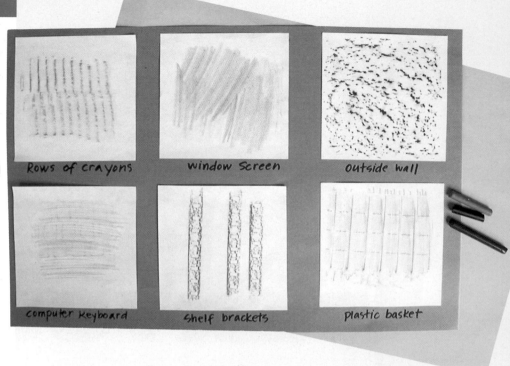

Rows of crayons • window screen • outside wall
computer keyboard • shelf brackets • plastic basket

Materials

- newsprint—5" (13 cm) squares
- dark-colored crayons without paper wrappers
- large piece of colored butcher paper
- glue

Step by Step

1. Ask students to name words that describe how things look and feel. List the words on the chalkboard or a chart. Sometimes it helps to think in terms of opposites when compiling the list.

rough	grainy
hard	bumpy
prickly	fluffy

2. Using the newsprint squares, have students do rubbings of different textures around the room.

3. Mount each rubbing on the butcher paper. Label each texture.

Hint

Have students categorize their texture rubbings according to the name words they listed.

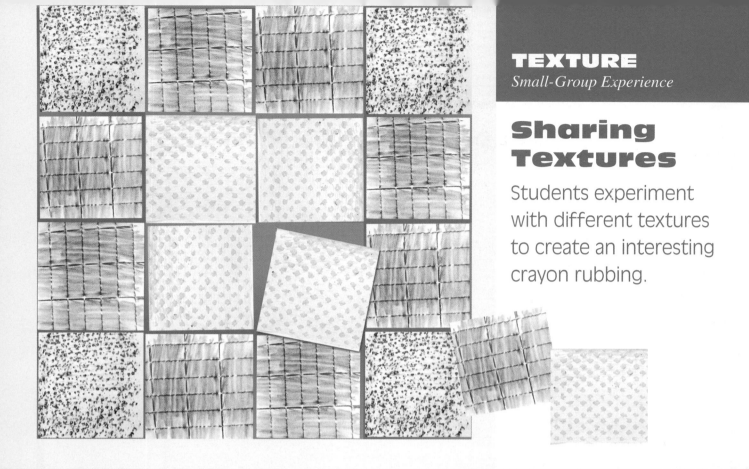

Sharing Textures

Students experiment with different textures to create an interesting crayon rubbing.

Step by Step

1. Divide the class into small groups.

2. Students meet in groups to plan the color palette for their texture rubbings. They record their decisions on their sheet.

3. Students do rubbings:
   • Locate a textured surface.
   • Choose a crayon in the color palette the group has chosen.
   • Make a rubbing on one of the small squares.

4. Students fold the butcher paper square into 16 squares.

5. Students arrange the textures on the butcher paper, placing one rubbing in each square. Glue the rubbings in place.

Materials
(for each group)

• colored butcher paper—
  24" (61 cm) square

• white construction paper—
  sixteen 5" (13 cm) squares

• crayons without paper wrappers

• glue

• Plan a Group Rubbing sheet on page 78

• surfaces with interesting textures

Reproduce this sheet to use with Sharing Textures on page 77.

Name ______________________________

Plan a Group Rubbing

Color Palette

Primary Colors

____
____
____

Cool

____
____
____

Secondary Colors

____
____
____

Warm

____
____
____

Complementary Colors

____
____
____

Other

____
____
____

Textures

____
____
____
____

Now make your rubbings. Experiment with different patterns. Then glue the squares in place in the pattern you like best.

On the Street Where I Live

Students enhance a drawing with crayon rubbings.

Step by Step

1. Students do simple pencil drawings of several houses along a street. The houses should have areas large enough for students to do rubbings inside the lines.

2. Students choose textures and do crayon rubbings to fill the inside area of each building.

3. Students outline the buildings and add details with black crayon or felt-tip pen.

Materials
(for each student)

• white construction paper—
  12" x 18" (30.5 x 46 cm)

• crayons

• pencil

• black crayon or felt-tip pen

Hint

Have students do crayon rubbings to fill each section of an accordion-folded fan.

Repetition Creates Texture

Texture can be created in pictures by using repetition of lines and shapes. This repetition creates a rhythm that holds the pattern together.

Materials

- construction paper— white 3" (7.5 cm) squares
- black crayons
- transparent tape

Step by Step

1. Discuss with students how different textures can be created by repeating a pattern. (You will need to show an example for each statement.)

   - One shape repeated over and over fills an area and creates a patterned effect.
   - Wavy lines drawn close together create movement and texture.
   - Cross-hatching adds shading and texture.
   - The distance between squiggles causes a change in the texture created.
   - Stippling (making tiny dots) can create texture.
   - Lines can be repeated in many variations. Lines and shapes repeated close together create a dark effect. Lines and shapes repeated farther apart create a lighter effect.

2. Give each student a 3" square of white construction paper. Have students use a black crayon to create a textured effect with a repeated line or shape.

3. Lay all of the squares in a line and tape them together with transparent tape.

4. Display the line of squares and discuss the different textures created.

Creating Texture with Paint

Students investigate painting techniques that create textured effects.

Step by Step

1. Demonstrate some of the techniques that create texture in a painting.
   dry brush
   thick brush vs. narrow brush
   splatter
   fingers
   stipple
   wavy
   toothbrush rubbed across screen
   overlaying or mixing colors

2. Show labeled examples of the techniques on the posterboard. Post the chart in the painting center.

3. Encourage students to experiment with different effects, adding new ones to the chart as they discover them.

Materials

• easel paper

• tempera paints

• several different-sized brushes

• assorted objects to use in creating textures: toothbrush, pencil, comb, plastic utensils, fingers, etc.

• posterboard

Hint

Fingers can make quite a variety of textures. Patting, dragging, and scribbling with both the finger and the fingernail is very effective.

Textured Paint Collage

Students cut apart textured paint papers they have created and make new simple collage pictures.

Materials

(for each student)

- white construction paper—

    4" x 6" (10 x 15 cm)

    three 4" (10 cm) squares

- acrylic paints
- flat-ended paintbrush
- scraps of cardboard
- plastic fork, plastic knife, comb (any object that will help to create a texture)
- scissors
- glue

Step by Step

1. Squeeze a small amount of paint onto each 4" square.

2. Allow students to experiment with creating different textures on each of their color squares.

3. Let the painted squares dry completely.

4. Brainstorm simple picture or design ideas that can be cut free-form from the squares.

5. Glue the shapes to the white construction paper.

Print a Texture

Sponges, potatoes, and gadgets are wonderful tools for printing texture and pattern in a picture.

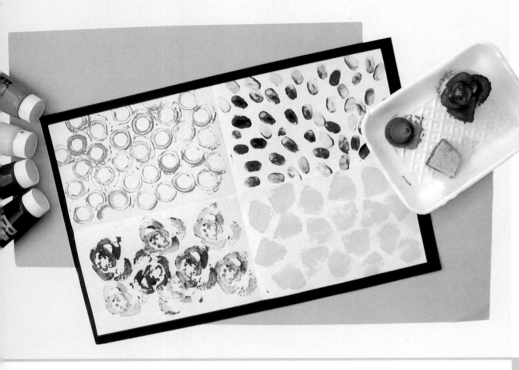

Step by Step

1. Students fold their construction paper into fourths.

2. Students make a different print of their choice in each area of the paper.

3. Dry paintings and discuss the textured effects created.

How to Make a Print

1. Pour a puddle of paint onto a flat container.

2. Dip one edge of an object into the paint.

3. Press the painted edge on the paper.

4. Lift the object straight up.

5. Repeat dipping, pressing, and lifting.

Materials

- white construction paper— 12" x 18" (30.5 x 46 cm)
- tempera paint in several colors
- sponges, potatoes, and gadgets
- foam meat trays or plates

Scratch-Away Texture

Students create a scratchboard painting.

Materials
(for each student)

- white construction paper—
  9" x 12" (23 x 30.5 cm)
- crayons
- black tempera paint
- liquid detergent
- paintbrush
- plastic knife

Step by Step

1. Students fill the white construction paper with color. The crayon lines should be thick and solid.

2. Students paint over the completed crayon design with a mixture of black tempera paint and a few drops of detergent.

3. Let the paint dry completely.

4. Students gently use the plastic knife to scratch away a design, revealing the color below.

This is a messy procedure. Cover tables or desks with plastic or newspaper to make cleanup easier.

A Collage Has Texture

A collage is a composition made by affixing pieces of paper, string, cloth, wallpaper, and other materials to a surface.

Step by Step

1. Students choose one piece of construction paper as a background.

2. Demonstrate several techniques for changing the texture of a collage.

   - Tear the paper and leave a torn edge.
   - Cut the paper.
   - Crinkle the paper and then smooth it out.
   - Score the paper and bend it.
   - Twist the paper.
   - Pleat the paper.
   - Weave the paper in and out.
   - Layer the paper.

3. Challenge students to use the other construction paper and the copy paper to create a collage. Encourage them to invent their own techniques to create texture.

4. Glue the pieces of paper to the background.

Materials
(for each student)

- construction paper—
  two 9" x 12" (23 x 30.5 cm)
  sheets (one each of two colors)

- sheet of copy paper

- scissors

- glue

Texture a Tree

Groups of students cooperate in creating trees, incorporating various techniques to add texture to their projects.

Materials
(for each group)

- white butcher paper—36" (91.5 cm) square
- assorted construction paper scraps
- assorted craft papers—paper bags, wallpaper, wrapping paper, tissue
- tempera paint in assorted colors
- brushes, sponges, and gadgets
- scissors
- white glue

Step by Step

1. Divide the class into groups of two to four students.

2. Explain the objective of the assignment—to create a tree using several different texture techniques. Have students brainstorm different types of trees that they might create.

   - blossoming trees
   - fruit trees
   - evergreen trees with pinecones
   - cactus
   - oak tree with acorns
   - tree with fall-colored leaves

3. Each group plans its tree and gathers materials. Students will need to assign specific jobs and work together to complete the job.

4. Have groups list all the texture techniques used on their trees.

5. Each tree is created on the butcher paper, cut out, and pinned to a bulletin board.

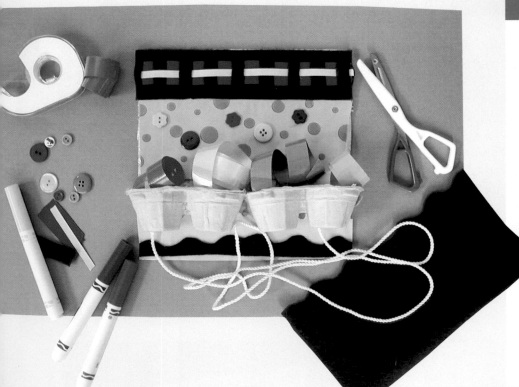

My Personal Collage

Students practice texture techniques to create a collage in an art center.

Step by Step

1. Review texture techniques with students. Remind them that they can tear paper, cut paper, overlap patterns, use paint plus torn paper, or use special scissors.

2. Students visit the art center to build a collage.

3. Plan a time for students to share their collages and explain any special texture technique they developed.

Hint

You can narrow the parameters of this experience by giving a specific topic.

- *Create a collage that represents Presidents' Day.*
- *Create a collage that shows your favorite pet.*

Materials

- 9" (23 cm) squares of cardboard for each student
- paper bags
- aluminum foil
- wallpaper scraps
- wrapping paper scraps
- colored papers
- packaging materials
- corrugated paper
- yarn
- cellophane
- tissue paper
- fabric
- egg cartons
- tempera paint
- brushes
- scissors

Animal Collage

Students create two animals in a collage. The animals are the same except one is a cut-paper design and the other is a torn-paper design.

Materials

(for each student)

- newsprint
- construction paper—
  white 12" x 18" (30.5 x 46 cm)
  scraps in assorted sizes and colors
- wallpaper, wrapping paper, paper bags, etc.
- crayons and felt-tip pens
- scissors
- white glue
- *Alexander and the Wind-up Mouse* by Leo Lionni; Pantheon

Step by Step

1. Read the story of *Alexander and the Wind-up Mouse.* This delightful fable serves as an example of cut versus torn-paper art. The "real" mouse in the story is created with a torn-paper edge. The mechanical mouse that becomes his friend is made with a cut-paper edge.

2. Students choose an animal for their collage. It is best if they can create their animal drawing out of simple, basic shapes. They draw the animal on the newsprint. Then they cut out the animal body parts.

3. Students trace these animal shapes onto construction paper. Each shape must be traced twice.

4. Students cut out one set of shapes and tear out the other set of shapes.

5. Students lay the shapes on a construction paper background and glue them in place.

6. Add additional paper pieces to create a background. Details may be added with crayons or felt-tip pens.

Cloth Collage

The different patterns and textures of cloth give students the opportunity to create varied and interesting collages.

Step by Step

1. Organize the materials in a center.

2. Students visit the center to choose their cloth. They will need to browse through the fabric to choose the combination of pieces they want to use together.

3. Students experiment with different arrangements. They may want to try tearing as well as cutting to create pieces of an appropriate size. Patterns may overlap or weave in and out.

4. When the arrangement is complete, the pieces are brushed with diluted white glue and placed on the cardboard.

Materials

• cloth scraps (as many colors, textures, and patterns as possible)

• 8" (20 cm) squares of cardboard

• scissors that will cut cloth

• white glue

Hint

Cloth is hard to cut with classroom scissors. You may want to provide precut strips, squares, and circles.

Sandpaper and Paint Collage

Students build in different textures by beginning their design with pieces of sandpaper.

Materials

- sandpaper—3" (7.5 cm) squares of different textures
- construction paper for each student—6" x 9" (15 x 23 cm)
- tempera paint in several colors
- sponges, brushes, and gadgets
- black marking pen
- glue

Step by Step

1. Students choose the sandpaper they will use. They glue it onto the construction paper or cut it into a shape before they glue it in place.

2. Students add paint. They may use brushes, sponges, or printing gadgets.

3. Dry the pictures completely. Add final details with a black marking pen.

Hint

Challenge students to use scraps of different-textured sandpaper to create a sandpaper-only collage.

Shape Rubbings

Students experiment with texture and color as they create this rubbing using one single shape.

Step by Step

1. Provide students with a variety of shape templates: stars, hearts, ovals, squares, etc.

2. Students tape the template of choice to the tabletop.

3. The white paper is placed over the template. Students rub on the paper with the side of the crayon in the spot where they can feel the template below. Suddenly the shape appears with a colored outline.

4. Student may then move the paper and rub with another color. The process is repeated over and over until they are happy with the result.

Materials

• white drawing paper—9" x 12" (23 x 30.5 cm)

• crayons with the papers removed

• shape templates cut from old file folders or tagboard

• two-sided tape

FORM

Learning About
FORM

When a flat, two-dimensional shape is bent, a third dimension is created. The shape becomes a form. Artists use form when they create sculptures.

Some forms commonly used are cylinders, cones, spheres, cubes, pyramids, and prisms.

What Is Form?

Investigate how form is created. Discuss the difference between two-dimensional and three-dimensional objects.

Materials

- three-dimensional objects: soup can, ball, box, prism, cardboard paper roll, etc.
- 4 1/4" x 11" (10.6 x 28 cm) piece of paper for each student
- tape

Step by Step

1. Show the can, ball, box, and prism to your students. Explain that each is a form because it has three dimensions.

2. Take a plain sheet of paper and ask the students if it is a form. The answer is no because it is flat or two-dimensional.

3. Roll the paper into a cylinder and ask the same question. The answer is now yes because you have added a dimension and made it three-dimensional.

4. Give each student a piece of paper and two pieces of tape. Challenge them to create a form out of the paper. If the students choose to, they may cut or tear their papers as they create their forms.

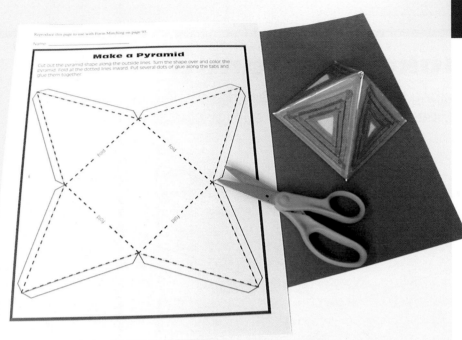

2-D to 3-D

Students change a two-dimensional shape into a three-dimensional form.

Step by Step

1. Students color the two-dimensional design and cut it out.

2. Students fold the pattern on the fold lines.

3. Students put a bit of glue on each tab and create the pyramid.

4. Discuss with students the difference between the two-dimensional shape and the three-dimensional form.

Materials

- scissors
- glue
- marking pens
- Make a Pyramid sheet on page 96, reproduced for individual students

Hint

Challenge students to create their own patterns for three-dimensional forms.

Name _____

Make a Pyramid

Cut out the pyramid shape along the outside lines. Turn the shape over and color the pyramid. Fold all the dotted lines inward. Put several dots of glue along the tabs and glue them together.

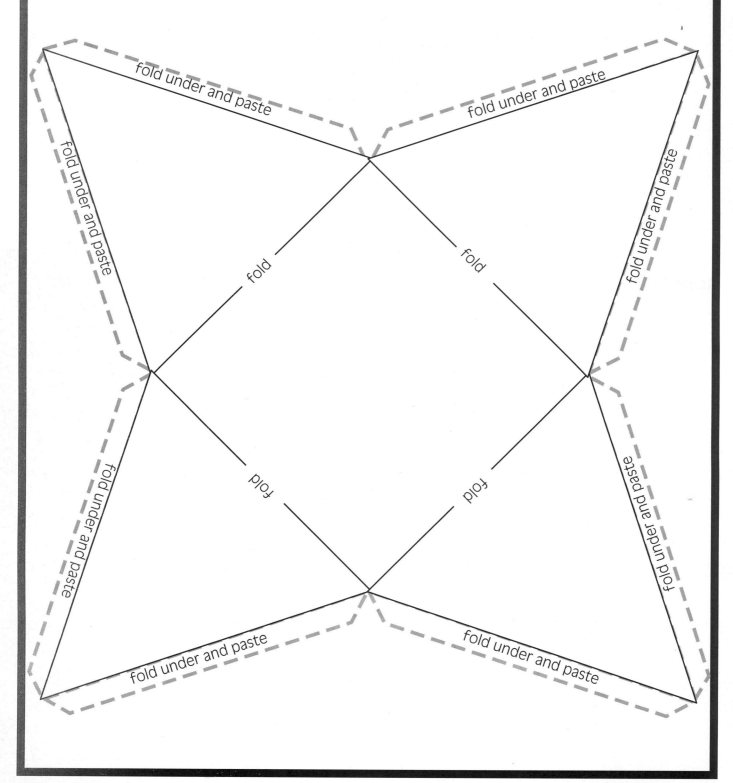

FORM
Center Experience

Making a Form

Students practice making forms out of modeling clay.

Step by Step

1. Show students how to use the clay. Develop guidelines to be followed when working with clay.

   For example:

   > *Clay stays on the work surface.*
   > *Put the clay back into its container when you are finished.*
   > *Clay is for modeling, not throwing.*

2. At the art center, have clay available for students to practice modeling basic forms: spheres, pyramids, boxes, cylinders, etc.

3. When a student has a completed form, the form is placed on a paper towel and labeled with his or her name for air-drying or firing. If you want to reuse the clay at the center, simply have students share their forms before putting the clay back into its container.

Hint

Try having students name each of the forms with a descriptive phrase.

a no-corner, smooth-all-over ball

Materials
(for each student)

- a fist-sized lump of clay
- flat surface for shaping clay
- paper towels

Pinch a Pot

One basic form that artists make is a bowl. Using a simple pinch technique, the students make their own bowls.

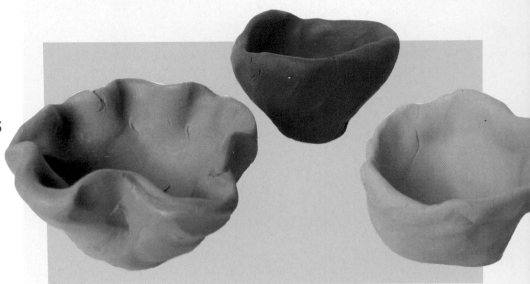

Materials
(for each student)

- 2" (5 cm) ball of clay
- flat surface for work

Step by Step

1. Give each student a ball of clay. Explain that it is important to keep the clay in one piece as the form is pinched.

2. Students stick their thumbs halfway into the clay balls.

3. With their thumbs still in the balls, students use their other four fingers to gently pinch the clay.

4. Students gently turn the ball while pinching it so that an even rim is formed.

5. Dry or bake the clay.

Hint
Use baker's clay to create the pinchpots. Bake the pots in the oven. Add colored accents with permanent markers and glaze.

Baker's Clay

- 1 cup (200 g) salt
- 1 ½ cups (360 ml) warm water
- 4 cups (500 g) flour

1. Mix salt and water.
2. Add to flour.
3. Stir until combined.
4. Knead at least five minutes.
5. Store in an airtight container.

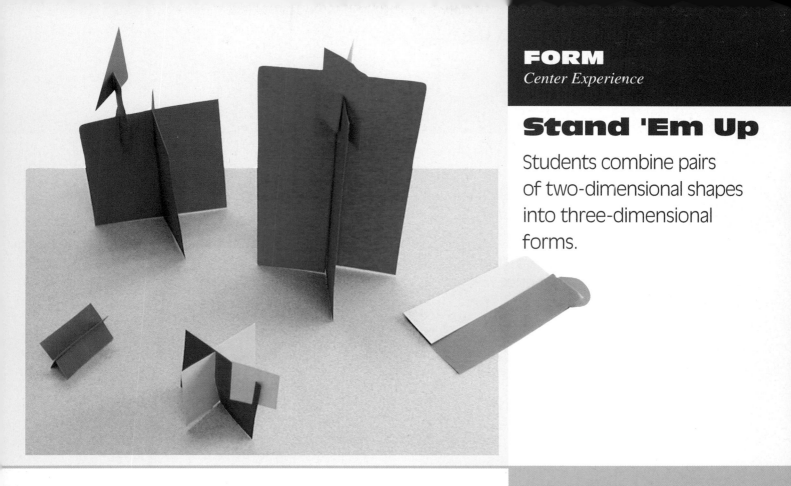

Stand 'Em Up

Students combine pairs
of two-dimensional shapes
into three-dimensional
forms.

Step by Step

1. Students cut two small identical squares or rectangles
   from construction paper. Shapes should not be larger than
   5" (13 cm) tall.

2. Students hold the two papers together and cut a slit halfway up.

3. Reversing one of the shapes, students slip one shape over the
   other to create a three-dimensional form.

4. Repeat, making several forms in different sizes and colors.

Materials

- brightly colored construction
  paper
- scissors

SPACE

99

Learning About

SPACE

Space in artwork makes a flat image look like it has form. There are several ways an artist adds space to artwork:

- Overlapping—Placing an object in front of another object makes the object in front appear closer than the one behind.

- Changing Size—An object that is smaller looks like it is in the distance while an object that is larger looks like it is closer.

- Using Perspective—Utilizing perspective, objects can be drawn on a flat surface to give an impression of their relative position and size.

Overlapping Collage

Students use both overlapping and size in creating space.

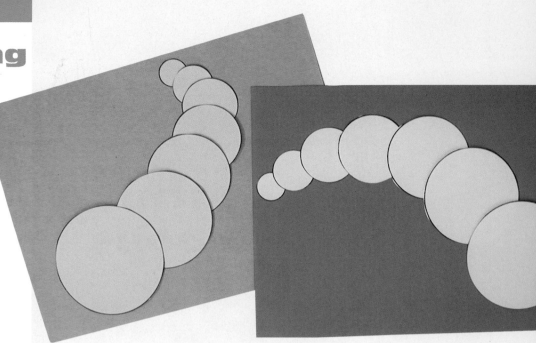

Materials

- circle patterns on page 103, reproduced on colored paper for individual students

- construction paper— 9" x 12" (23 x 30.5 cm), assorted colors

- scissors

- glue

- crayons

Step by Step

1. Each student cuts out the different-sized circles on the pattern sheet.

2. Students choose a contrasting color page for the background.

3. Students arrange their circles on the background paper using overlapping and size to create the illusion that the ball is coming toward the viewer.

4. Discuss the techniques students found to create the illusion. They should include these ideas:

   - The smallest circle should be the farthest away and in back.
   - The next smallest circle will overlap a small part of the previous circle.

5. Students rearrange their circles if necessary and glue them in place.

6. Students may use crayons to decorate the largest ball.

Reproduce this sheet on colored paper to use with Overlapping Collage on page 102.

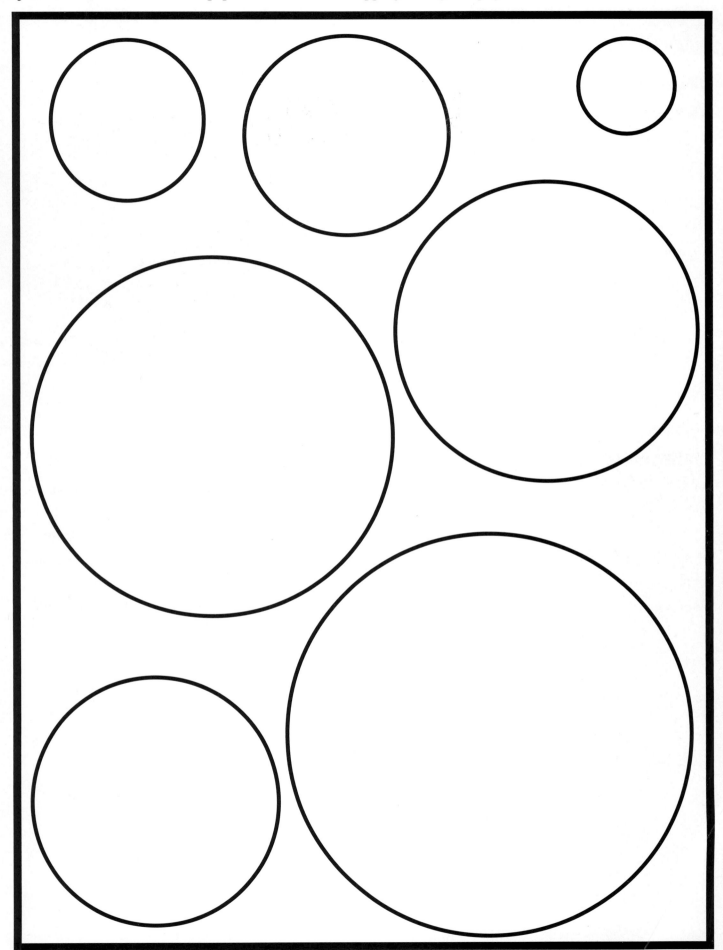

Perspective, One-Point!

Perspective is a tool artists use to create space in their artwork. This time students will experiment with one-point perspective.

Materials
(for each student)

- 8 1/2" x 11" (21.5 x 28 cm) sheet of drawing paper
- ruler
- pencil
- eraser

Step by Step

1. Students trace the horizon line parallel to the top and bottom of the paper.

2. Students place a dot on the horizon line. This is the **vanishing point**.

3. Students draw a shape with corners anywhere on the paper.

4. Students use the ruler to connect the corners of the shape to the vanishing point. If the line would have to go across the shape, it is not drawn.

5. Students draw the backside of the shape parallel to the front of the shape.

6. Erase the lines beyond the shape that connect to the vanishing point.

7. Encourage students to shade their shapes in different values of color.

Note: Use this with grades 4 through 6.

A Sunny Day

Students layer cutouts to show which object is closest.

Step by Step

1. Students cut shapes from the colored rectangles.
   - yellow—sun
   - green—top of a tree
   - red—house
   - blue—stairs
2. Students use colored paper scraps to add details to the cutouts.
3. Students layer the cutouts on the black paper. The farthest away should be in the back. Glue in place.

Materials
(for each student)

- construction paper—
  black 6" x 12" (15 x 30.5 cm)
  4" x 6" (10 x 15 cm)—one each: yellow, green, red, blue
- scissors
- glue

Hint
Have students create an original scene using four new cutouts.

A City in Perspective

Students use one-point perspective to create a cityscape that looks 3-D.

Materials

(for each student)

- construction paper—white 12" x 18" (30.5 x 46 cm)
- ruler
- pencil
- colored markers

Step by Step

1. Students draw a horizontal line about 2" (5 cm) from the bottom of the paper.

2. Along the line, students draw at least five different rectangles for building fronts.

3. Students draw a vanishing point on the top edge of the paper.

4. Students connect the corners of the buildings to the vanishing point. If a line goes through a building, students do not draw it.

5. Students add the backs and sides of the buildings by making lines parallel to the front lines.

6. Students erase the extra lines that continue to the vanishing point.

7. Students add details to the buildings: windows, doors, signs, shingles, chimneys, antennas, etc.

8. Students trace the pencil lines carefully with the black marker.

9. Students use colored markers to add color to the buildings.

Using the Elements of Art

Artists use seven elements of art in different ways in their art. Part Two of *How to Teach Art to Children* focuses on 24 famous artists and cultures. An accompanying activity allows the student to experience the style of each artist.

How to Use Part Two

The following experiences help students see how famous artists from ancient times to the present have used the basic elements of art to express themselves.

The Experiences

There are 24 experiences in Part Two of *How to Teach Art to Children*. Each experience is based on the work of a famous artist and includes the following components:

- a brief background statement about the artist
- a list of the art elements that are the focal point of the experience
- literature references for learning more about the artist
- a list of materials needed
- step-by-step directions for the experience

Using the Experiences

Follow these simple steps to use the experiences:

- Choose the experiences you want to use. The simplest ones are presented first, but all can be adapted to the appropriate level for your students.
- Gather examples of the featured artist's work. Books and magazines, museum catalogs, and Web galleries are great resources.
- Explain the experience to your students. Encourage creativity.
- Allow time for the thoughtful completion of the experiences.
- Discuss your students' experiences and how they might parallel those of the famous artist.
- Display finished art.

Resources for Teaching

The American Eye: Eleven Artists of the Twentieth Century by Jan Greenberg; Delacorte Press, 1995.

Art Revolutions: Pop Art by Linda Bolton; Peter Bedrick Books, 2000.

Art Revolutions: Surrealism by Linda Bolton; Peter Bedrick Books, 2000.

The Art of Shapes: For Children and Adults by Margaret Steele and Cindy Estes; Fotofolio, 1997.

A Child's Book of Art: Discover Great Paintings by Lucy Micklethwait; DK Publishing, 1999.

Discovering Great Artists: Hands-On Art for Children in the Styles of the Great Masters by MaryAnn F. Kohl; Bright Ring Publishing, 1997.

The Elements of Pop-Up: A Pop-Up Book for Aspiring Paper Engineers by David A. Carter and James Diaz; Little Simon, 1999.

Katie and the Mona Lisa by James Mayhew; Orchard Books, 1999.

Katie Meets the Impressionists by James Mayhew; Orchard Books, 1999.

Lives of the Artists: Masterpieces, Messes (And What the Neighbors Thought) by Kathleen Krull; Harcourt Brace, 1995.

When Pigasso Met Mootisse by Nina Laden; Chronicle Books, 1998.

The University of Michigan maintains a Web site that contains links to many wonderful online art resources:

www.umich.edu/~histart/mother/

Twittering Machines

Materials

- photograph of Paul Klee's *Twittering Machine*

For each student:

- construction paper—white 12" x 18" (30.5 x 46 cm)
- black crayon
- watercolor paints
- water containers
- paintbrushes

1

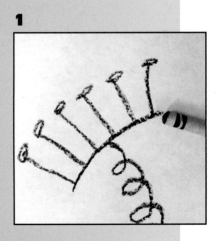

2

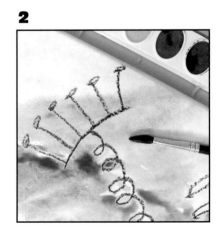

3

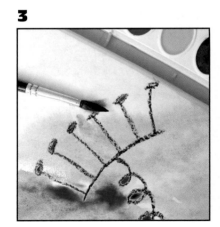

Art Elements

Line

Shape

Color

Talk About...

Show the students Paul Klee's *Twittering Machine*. Talk with the students about Paul Klee and his love for music. Ask:

• What kind of music do you think the twittering machine plays?

• If you could create your own twittering machine, what kinds of sounds might it make?

• What would it look like?

• What kinds of colors did Paul Klee use in this artwork?

Step by Step

1. Give each student paper and a black crayon. Challenge them to design their own twittering machines. They use lines and shapes to draw their machines. Then they elaborate and add lots of extra details.

2. Using the paintbrushes and water, students wet the entire paper. Then students drop in cool colors. The drops will spread out on the wet paper and blend together. Let the paintings dry.

3. Students add just a little bit of a warm color to the inside of some of the shapes. Let the paintings dry again.

4. Students sign their artwork and it is ready to display.

Paul Klee

Paul Klee was a German-Swiss painter who lived from 1879 to 1940. He loved music and played the violin. He was interested in creating a deep meaning in his art by using symbols. He was very imaginative in his works. His work called **Twittering Machine** hangs in The Museum of Modern Art in New York. This work is a pen-and-ink drawing with watercolor. It depicts an imaginary machine that looks like it may make music when the handle is turned.

Literature References

Dreaming Pictures: Paul Klee (Adventures in Art) by Paul Klee and Jurgen Von Schemm; Prestel USA, 1997.

Paul Klee (Getting to Know the World's Greatest Artists) by Mike Venezia; Children's Press, 1991.

Paul Klee (The Life and Work of) by Sean Connolly; Heinemann Library, 1999.

Prints

Materials

- example of Piet Mondrian's artwork

For each student:

- thick string
- piece of cardboard—8" x 10" (20 x 25.5 cm)
- scissors
- masking tape
- black paint
- paintbrush
- construction paper—white 8" x 10" (20 x 25.5 cm)
- drying rack
- red, yellow, and blue crayons

2

3

4

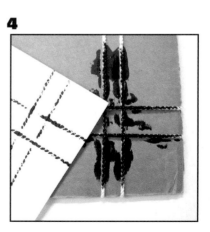

Art Elements

Line

Shape

Color

Talk About...

Show the example of Piet Mondrian's artwork and ask the students to describe it. Ask:

• What colors do you see?

• What kinds of lines? How are the lines placed?

• What shapes? Is this a picture of something you recognize?

Step by Step

1. Give each student a piece of cardboard and paper, several yards of string, and several pieces of tape.

2. Students should wrap a total of five pieces of string around their boards, both vertically and horizontally. Cut the string and tape the ends on the back to keep the string tightly in place. This becomes a printing plate.

3. Paint the string with black paint. This process is called *inking the printing plate.*

4. Position the printing plate paint-side down above the white paper. Press it down to print the image of the black lines onto the paper. Lift it straight up.

5. Place the prints on a drying rack to dry.

6. Look again at Piet Mondrian's artwork. Ask the students to notice if every shape is colored. Ask if all the colored shapes are right next to each other or spread apart.

7. Using the crayons, students fill in three shapes with yellow, two with red, and four with blue. The colored shapes should be spread out just like in Mondrian's paintings.

Piet Mondrian

Piet Mondrian was born in 1872 and lived until 1944. He worked to create his own simple style of painting, and in the early 1900s he evolved his very modern style. Mondrian used only vertical and horizontal straight lines and the three primary colors (red, yellow, and blue) with black and white.

Literature References

Piet Mondrian by Hans Ludwig C. Jaffe; Harry N. Abrams, 1986.

Piet Mondrian 1872–1944: Structures in Space by Susanne Deicher; TASCHEN America Llc., 1996.

Sunflowers

Materials

- photograph of one of Vincent Van Gogh's paintings showing sunflowers in a vase

For each student:

- construction paper

  background—blue 9" x 12" (23 x 30.5 cm)

  vase—yellow 6" x 9" (15 x 23 cm)

  sunflower center— orange 3" (7.5 cm) square

  stem—green 1" x 6" (2.5 x 15 cm)

- tissue paper—yellow, red, and orange, torn in strips
- dried black beans
- scissors
- glue
- chalk—light-colored and orange
- toilet paper

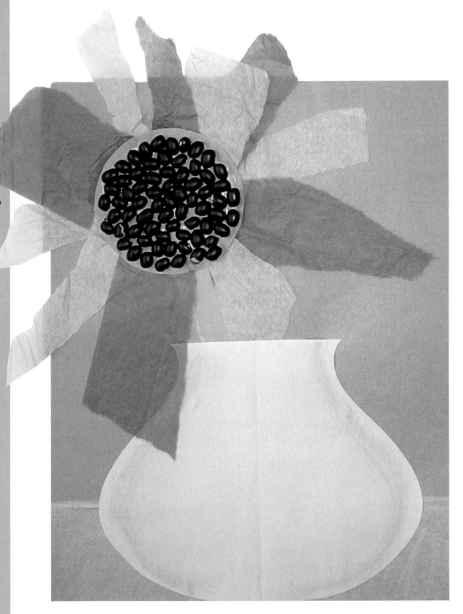

2a

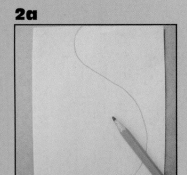

2b

3, 4

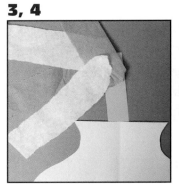

5, 7

Art Elements

Line

Shape

Color

Texture

Space

Talk About...

Discuss an example of Vincent Van Gogh's *Sunflowers*. Ask:

• What colors did Van Gogh use in the background?

• What about the sunflowers? The vase?

• Are the colors warm or cool?

Step by Step

1. On the piece of blue construction paper, students draw a line one-fourth up from the bottom with light chalk and fill in the table area below the line. Blend with toilet paper.

2. Students cut out a vase shape from the yellow construction paper and lay it on their blue background. Using a piece of orange chalk, students make a line down the side of the vase. They rub the chalk line with toilet paper to create a shadow effect. The chalk shadow helps to create an illusion of space.

3. Position the green construction paper strip stem in the vase.

4. Students arrange the tissue strips in a flower shape on the background paper.

5. Students round the corners of the orange square to make the sunflower center. Lay it on top of the tissue strips.

6. Glue the petals, stem, flower center, and vase in place.

7. Students glue black beans onto the sunflower center. The beans add the texture.

8. Artists sign their artwork and admire the beautiful sunflowers!

Vincent Van Gogh

Vincent Van Gogh (1853–1890) is famous for his use of raw color and wild brushstrokes. He became a painter after failing at many other careers. He painted day and night. He would set up still life arrangements to paint indoors when he couldn't paint outside. He painted his food, his shoes, and sunflowers in vases. His sunflowers are fun to look at, with their wild, bright-yellow petals and their large dark centers. The vase he placed them in was also bright and yellow.

Literature References

Camille and the Sunflowers: A Story About Vincent Van Gogh by Laurence Anholt; Barron's Juveniles, 1994.

The First Starry Night by Joan Shaddox Isom; Charlesbridge Publishing, 1998.

Painting the Wind by Michelle Dionetti; Little, Brown and Company Inc., 1996.

Van Gogh (Basic Art) edited by Taschen; TASCHEN America Llc., 2000.

Clay Cartouches

Materials

- an example of a cartouche containing hieroglyphs

For each student:

- hieroglyphic alphabet on page 118
- oval cartouche pattern on page 119
- dull pencil
- clay
- paper clip
- brown tempera paint
- paintbrush
- paper towels

1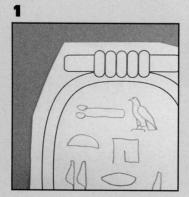

2

3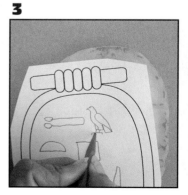

4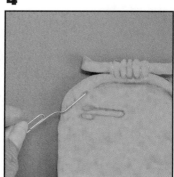

Art Elements

Line

Shape

Talk About...

Show the example of the hieroglyphs. Relate the hieroglyphs to the alphabet. Point out the cartouche in the picture. Explain that the cartouche spells a name.

Step by Step

1. Have the students place their oval cartouche pattern over the hieroglyphic alphabet paper and trace the characters that spell their name.

2. They turn the pattern over and scribble with pencil on the backside. This creates a form of carbon paper so that when the pattern is placed on the clay, they can trace over the lines and transfer the symbols onto the clay.

3. Roll out a 1/4" (0.6 cm) thick layer of clay. Proceed to trace over the pattern and hieroglyphs with a dull pencil to transfer the design onto the clay.

4. Use the paper clip to cut away the extra clay along the outside of the cartouche pattern. Then reinforce the pencil lines with the paper clip.

5. Let the clay dry and then fire, bake it, or set up the clay as directed by the manufacturer.

6. Students paint the entire cartouche with a thin layer of brown paint.

7. Students quickly wipe off the paint with a paper towel so that it remains only in the crevices.

Ancient Egyptians

In ancient times, Egyptians used hieroglyphs to write messages in stone and on papyrus. The hieroglyphs (pictures and symbols) used by the Egyptians were their alphabet. By combining the pictures, the Egyptians could spell out words. On the walls of the pyramids, the messages contain groups of hieroglyphs that are surrounded by an oval. These ovals with hieroglyphs in them are called cartouches. The hieroglyphs inside a cartouche spell a name.

Literature References

Ancient Egyptian Designs for Artists and Craftspeople by Eva Wilson; Dover Publications, 1989.

Egyptian Designs (Dover Pictorial Archive) by Carol Belanger Grafton; Dover Publications, 1993.

Fun with Hieroglyphs by Catharine Roehrig; Penguin USA, 1990.

Hieroglyphs from A to Z: A Rhyming Book with Ancient Egyptian Stencils for Kids by Peter Der Manuelian; Scholastic Trade, 1996.

Pyramids: 50 Hands-On Activities to Experience Ancient Egypt by Avery Hart and Paul Mantell; Williamson Publishing, 1997.

Reproduce this sheet for students to use with Clay Cartouches on page 117.

Hieroglyphic Alphabet

a		h		o		v	
b		i		p		w	
c		j		q		x	
d		k		r		y	
e		l		s		z	
f		m		t		boy	
g		n		u		girl	

Reproduce this pattern for students to use with Clay Cartouches on page 117.

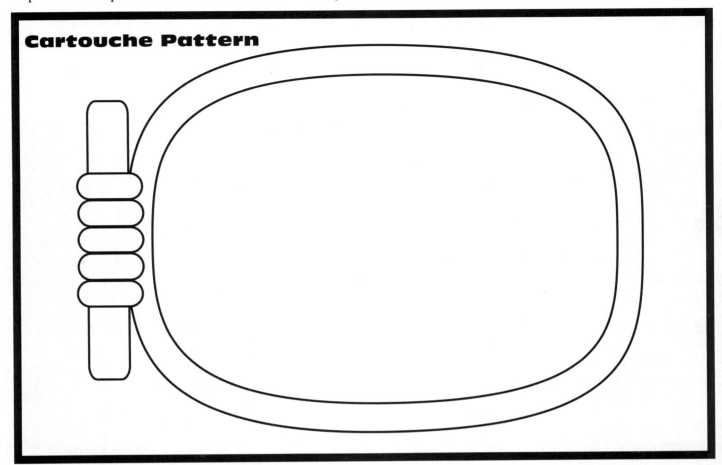

Cartouche Pattern

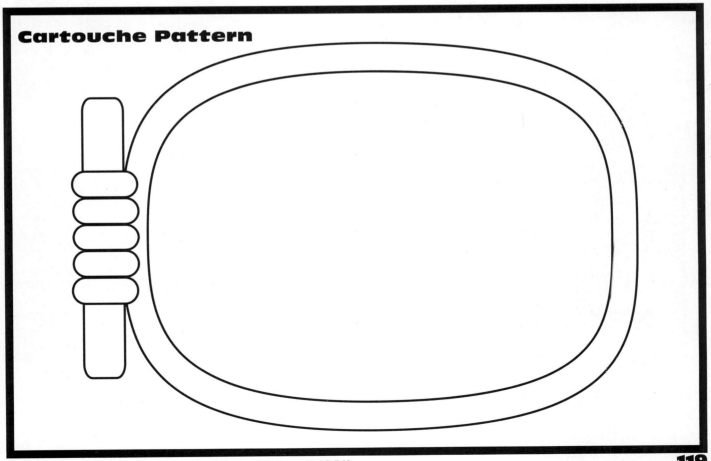

Cartouche Pattern

Adinkra Cloth

Materials

- sample or picture of Adinkra cloth

For each student:

- construction paper—brown 9" (23 cm) square
- ruler
- black crayon
- gadgets to print with (objects that you have collected that will make an interesting image when inked and then stamped)
- black printing ink or tempera paint
- washable, portable flat surface or plate

1

2a

2b

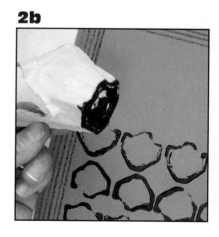

This project uses the design of an Adinkra cloth, substituting gadget prints for the elaborate stamps made by the Ashanti peoples.

©2001 by Evan-Moor Corp. • How to Teach Art to Children • EMC 760

Art Elements

Line

Shape

Talk About...

Talk to the students about Adinkra cloth and the Ashanti peoples. Find Ghana on a map or globe. Ask the students if they notice anything in the Adinkra cloth (lines, shapes, repeated patterns).

Step by Step

1. Each student uses the ruler and black crayon to make a border of straight lines around the construction paper square.

2. Students choose a gadget and print the same object in a repeating pattern on their square.

   • Pour a puddle of paint or ink on a flat surface or plate.
   • Spread the paint or ink into an even layer.
   • Place the gadget to be printed in the paint.
   • Press the paint edge of the gadget onto the paper.
   • Lift straight up.

3. Once the squares are printed, let the paint dry completely. The squares may be combined to create a class Adinkra cloth. You may want to add multicolored ribbon to represent the colorful stitches used to hold the strips of Adinkra cloth together.

Ashanti Peoples

Adinkra cloth is made by the Ashanti peoples in Ghana, Africa. They use black ink to print symbols with different meanings on fabric. They make stamps out of gourds. Then they apply ink to the stamps and press them on the fabric. They may separate squares of the designs with lines. The Ashanti often sew the pieces of cloth together with brightly colored thread to make clothes for special ceremonies.

Literature References

African Designs from Traditional Sources by Geoffrey Williams; Dover Publications, 1971.

Traditional African Designs by Gregory Mirow; Dover Publications, 1997.

West African Symbols: Adinkra: 31 Rubber Stamps by Mimi Robinson; Chronicle Books, 1998.

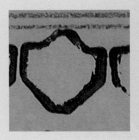

Pop-up Collage Cards

Materials

- examples of Henri Matisse's paper collages

For each student:

- construction paper—
  white 9" x 12"
  (23 x 30.5 cm)

  scraps in various colors
- scissors
- glue
- pencil

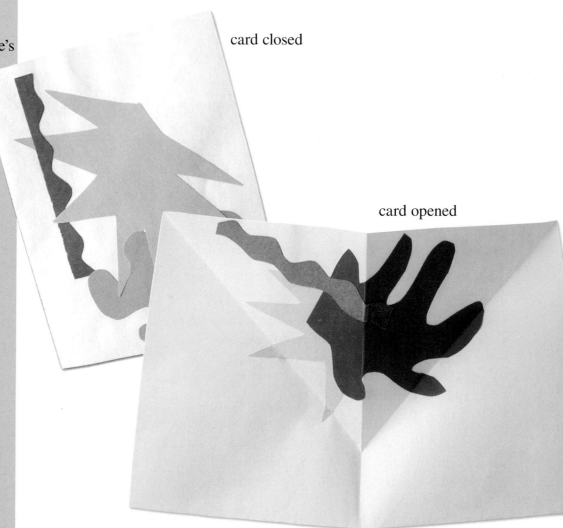

card closed

card opened

2a, b, c

2e

2g

2h

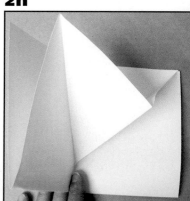

Art Elements

Shape

Color

Form

Talk About...

Talk about Matisse's cutouts and the reason he began doing cutouts rather than paintings. Have students note the shapes in the collages. Also ask students to notice the colors that Matisse used.

Step by Step

1. Give students white background paper.

2. Have students fold their papers to make a pop-up card.
   a. Fold the paper in half lengthwise.
   b. Fold the top corner (fold side) down to the open edge.
   c. Turn the paper over and reverse the fold.
   d. Open the paper.
   e. Pull the top center fold inside and to the left side of the page. Press folds firmly.
   f. Open the paper again.
   g. Fold the bottom to meet the top. Press fold firmly.
   h. Close the card so that the plain side is outside and the triangle fold is inside. Press firmly again.

3. Have students choose three colors of paper scraps. Students cut out and arrange shapes on the inside and outside of their cards.

4. Once the shapes are arranged, use dots of glue to attach the shapes to the card. Let the glue dry.

Henri Matisse

Henri Matisse (1869–1954) painted large vibrant canvases in his early career. Later in his life, Matisse became ill and was confined to a wheelchair. Because he could no longer stand up at his canvases, he began to cut out paper designs and arrange them in attractive compositions. His *Jazz* series is very famous.

Literature References

A Bird or Two: A Story About Henri Matisse by Bijou Le Tord; Wm. B. Eerdmans Publishing Co., 1999.

Matisse (Famous Artists) by Antony Mason, Andrew S. Hughes, and Jen Green; Barron's Juveniles, 1995.

Drawing an Invention

Materials

- examples of Leonardo da Vinci's invention drawings

For each student:

- newsprint
- manila paper— 9" x 12" (23 x 30.5 cm)
- pencil
- eraser
- ruler
- brown marking pen
- brown butcher or construction paper

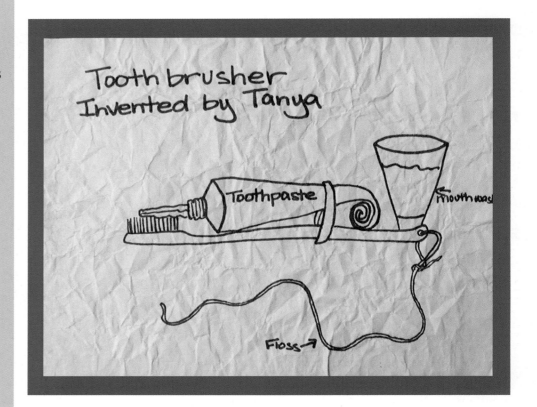

4

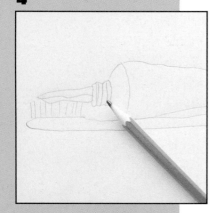

5

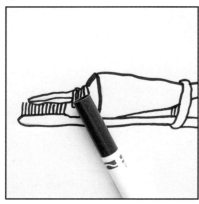

6

Art Elements

Line

Shape

Texture

Talk About...

Have the students look at examples of Leonardo da Vinci's drawings. Ask them what they think the different machines might do. Does it look as if Leonardo da Vinci took time to draw these inventions or did he just scribble them out? Have students think about what invention they would make to help them in their lives.

Step by Step

1. Tell students that they are now inventors like Leonardo da Vinci. They are to draw a machine that will help them do something. On the practice paper, have students draw three different ideas. Artists always come up with more than one idea!

2. Help students choose one of their drawings or urge them to combine several of their ideas together in one machine.

3. Once students have chosen their machines, give them their manila paper.

4. Students draw their machines in pencil on their paper. They may add written instructions on their paper as well.

5. Students trace over their pencil lines with brown marker.

6. Students add texture to their paper to make it look old by crumpling it and uncrumpling it several times.

7. Mount the drawings on brown paper and display the creative ideas.

Leonardo da Vinci

Leonardo da Vinci (1452–1519) is a well-known artist and inventor. He was born in Italy in 1452. Leonardo da Vinci was known as a "Renaissance Man." He loved learning. He not only painted one of the world's most famous portraits, *Mona Lisa*, but he also made many contributions to science. He was an inventor too. Leonardo da Vinci's drawings included ideas for many different inventions. He was always thinking! He even wrote backwards to keep people from stealing his ideas!

Literature References

Da Vinci (Getting to Know the World's Greatest Artists) illustrated by Mike Venezia; Children's Press, 1994.

Da Vinci: The Painter Who Spoke with Birds (Art for Children) by Yves Pinguilly; Chelsea House Publishers, 1994.

Leonardo da Vinci by Diane Stanley; HarperCollins Juvenile Books, 2000.

Circus Mobiles

Materials

- photographs of Alexander Calder's mobiles
- pictures of circus animals

For each student:

- colored construction paper
- pencil
- scissors
- crayons
- hole punch
- string or thread
- wire hanger

3

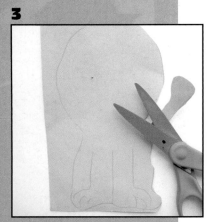

4, 5

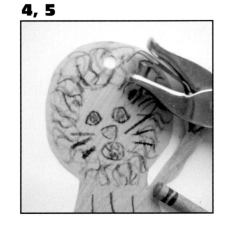

6, 7

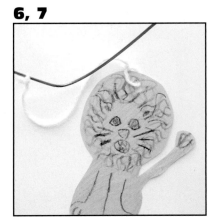

Art Elements

Line

Shape

Color

Form

Talk About...

Talk with the students about the circus. Show a picture of Alexander Calder's *Wire Circus.* Ask students to notice details in the sculpture. Show some of Calder's later sculptures. Ask the students to compare Calder's early work with his later work. What are the differences? What is the same? Do they see lines, shape, color, and form?

Step by Step

1. Display pictures of circus animals and symbols around the room. Have students choose 5 of their favorites.

2. Students choose a piece of construction paper and draw their animals and/or symbols in pencil.

3. Students cut out their animals.

4. Using crayons, students add details to their animals on both sides.

5. They punch a hole in the top of each animal.

6. Students thread strings through the holes.

7. Using wire hangers to create bases for the mobiles, students tie the animals to the hanger bases. (There should be an odd number of animals on each mobile.)

8. Hang up the mobiles to display the students' work.

Alexander Calder

Alexander Calder (1898–1976) is famous for his kinetic sculptures or mobiles. In his early work, Calder created a circus out of wire that reminded him of the fun he had as a child. His later works used shapes and wire together to create whimsical moving sculptures. These later sculptures represent animals or objects.

Literature References

Alexander Calder (Getting to Know the World's Greatest Artists) by Mike Venezia; Children's Press, 1998.

Ballerina Paintings

Materials

- examples of Edgar Degas' ballerinas
- tutu and ballerina shoes for model

For each student:

- white paper—12" x 18" (30.5 x 46 cm)
- pencil
- eraser
- thin black marking pen
- oil pastels
- tempera paint—brown, green, blue, and purple
- paintbrushes

2, 3, 4

5, 6, 7

8

Art Elements

Line

Color

Talk About...

Show examples of Degas' ballerinas. Ask students to describe details about the dancers. Ask them if they have ever seen a ballerina.

Step by Step

1. Choose a student to be the first model. Have the model put on the tutu and shoes. The model should pretend to be dancing and strike a pose.

2. Students draw the model quickly in pencil. Have them use light pressure on the paper so they can erase if they need to.

3. Students add details to the dancer.

4. Students draw in a line for the back of the stage.

5. Students carefully trace over all lines with a black marking pen.

6. Students carefully paint the stage brown, leaving the ballerina unpainted.

7. Students paint the background a cool color (green, blue, or purple), again being careful not to paint over the ballerina. Let paint dry.

8. Show the students how to use oil pastels. Have them color in their ballerinas with oil pastels. Use a skin color on skin and whatever color they want for the costume, hair, and eyes.

Edgar Degas

Edgar Degas (1834–1917) is famous for his paintings of ballerinas. He painted with Claude Monet during the impressionist movement. However, Degas did not use short brushstrokes like Monet. Degas preferred to use a more realistic style. The dancers in Degas' paintings look like they might have been photographed. Degas was able to capture a single moment in his paintings and save it for many people to look at.

Literature References

Degas and the Little Dancer: A Story About Edgar Degas by Laurence Anholt; Barron's Juveniles, 1996.

Edgar Degas (Getting to Know the World's Greatest Artists) illustrated by Mike Venezia; Children's Press, 2000.

Accordion Books

Materials

For each student:

- tagboard—two red 4" x 5" (10 x 13 cm) pieces
- construction paper— white 4 3/4" x 15" (11.5 x 38 cm)
- stamp with different shapes made from foam material, mounted on a wooden block or jar lid
- gold tempera paint
- flat surface or plate
- glue
- 20" (51 cm) black ribbon or yarn
- pencil
- crayons
- black marking pen

1

2

3

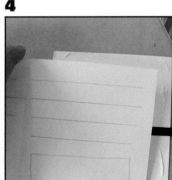

4

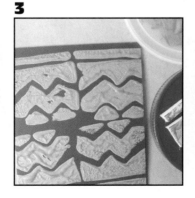

Art Elements

Line

Shape

Color

Talk About...

Discuss the history of bound books. Be sure to mention China and the invention of accordion books. Tell the students that they are going to make their very own accordion book.

Step by Step

1. Students fold the long white paper into accordion pages.

   • First, fold the paper in half.

   • Next, fold the top end back to meet the fold and crease a new fold.

   • Turn the paper over and do the same on the other side.

2. Each student creates a stamp by cutting foam material in a repeating design. Glue the pieces to a wooden block or jar lid.

3. Students press their stamps into the gold paint and print a pattern on their red tagboard covers. Let the paint dry thoroughly.

4. Students put the books together.

   • Lay the back cover with the decorated side touching the table.

   • Lay the ribbon or yarn so the middle of it is in the middle of the back cover.

   • Glue on the back end of the accordion-folded white paper and lay it down on the cover.

   • Place a few drops of glue on the front end of the accordion pages and place the top cover on the book with the printed side facing out.

5. The books are finished and ready for filling with wonderful stories or to use as a personal journal. Lines may be lightly penciled in for writing, or students may use this book as a sketch pad for their drawings.

Chinese Bookmakers

Books with hard covers like those found in a library were first made in China.

• Before the invention of hard covers, long strips of paper were rolled into scrolls.

• These long strips of paper evolved into accordion books with hard covers.

• Later, the edges of the hard covers were sewn together on one side.

The Chinese also created a printing process that used carved blocks of wood to print images in books.

One strong symbol in the Chinese culture is the dragon. It stands for truth, life, power, nobility, and fortune. The dragon is often gold, green, or red, or a combination of all three colors.

Literature References

Behold...the Dragons! by Gail Gibbons; Morrow Junior, 1999.

Mouse Match by Ed Young; Silver Whistle, 1997.

Story Quilts

Materials

- *Tar Beach* by Faith Ringgold

For each student:

- construction paper—white 12" x 18" (30.5 x 46 cm)
- wrapping paper or wallpaper 1 1/2" (4 cm) squares
- glue
- black marking pen
- pencil
- eraser
- crayons and colored chalk
- toilet paper
- ruler

1, 2

3, 4, 5

6, 7, 8

Art Elements

Line

Shape

Color

Talk About...

Read the book *Tar Beach* to the students and have them look at the illustrations. Explain to them that Faith Ringgold's paintings were quilts. Ask them to look for the lines where the paintings are sewn. Also ask them to notice the quilted borders of her paintings. What kind of colors do they notice in the paintings?

Step by Step

1. Each student starts with white drawing paper. Using contrasting colors next to each other, students glue different squares of patterned wallpaper or wrapping paper around their papers to create a "quilted" border.

2. Students use a black marking pen to add little stitches around the squares to look like a quilt.

3. In pencil, the students lightly draw a picture and write a story in the center of the quilted paper. Students may use a ruler to keep their writing aligned.

4. Students color their illustrations with crayons. They should use a lot of bright colors like Faith Ringgold uses!

5. Students may trace over their penciled-in story with marking pen.

6. Using a piece of chalk in a cool color (blue, green, or purple), students lightly rub color into the background around the image. (Note: Use just a light rubbing of color.)

7. Use some toilet paper to blend in the color.

8. Have the students sign their quilts and then share them with the class.

Faith Ringgold

Faith Ringgold is an important African-American artist. She was born in Harlem, New York, in 1930. Her artwork has a fun, imaginative quality. Most of her works are quilted paintings. She paints on canvas and then quilts a border to sew on the edges. Quilted paintings were photographed for the illustrations in her book *Tar Beach*. Faith Ringgold often includes herself and people she knows in her paintings.

Literature References

Talking to Faith Ringgold by Faith Ringgold; Crown Publishing, 1995.

Tar Beach by Faith Ringgold; Crown Publishing, 1991.

Still Lifes

Materials

- example of a still life painted by Paul Cézanne
- white tablecloth, tall vase, and various fruits

For each student:

- construction paper—
  - blue 11" x 17" (28 x 43 cm)
  - white 6" x 17" (15 x 43 cm)
  - gray 5" x 7" (13 x 18 cm)
  - scraps of warm colors
- scissors
- glue
- black and white chalk
- toilet paper

2

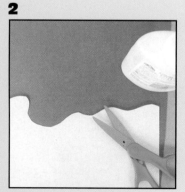

3

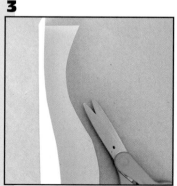

4

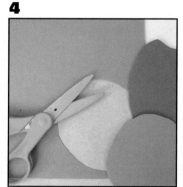

5

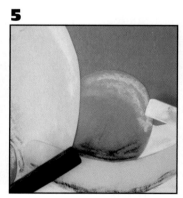

Art Elements

Line

Shape

Color

Value

Space

Form

Talk About...

Discuss Paul Cézanne and his artwork with the students. Show one of his still life paintings and ask students to tell what they think a still life is. Ask students to notice the values (lights and darks) in Cézanne's paintings.

Step by Step

1. Set up a still life with a white tablecloth, a tall vase, and various fruits.

2. Students make the tablecloth.

   • Using scissors, students cut one wavy edge to represent the folds along the top of the tablecloth.

   • Students glue the tablecloth to the blue background paper.

3. Students cut out a vase from the gray paper. The vase may be cut on a folded sheet of paper so that it is symmetrical.

4. Students cut out colored fruit and arrange the vase and fruit on their tablecloths. By overlapping the shapes, the students create space. Once they are happy with their composition, they glue their shapes in place.

5. Show the students how to use the black chalk on one side of the shapes (vase and fruit) and the white chalk on the other side of the shapes to add form to the flat shapes. Explain that they are using value just like Cézanne did in his still life paintings. Blend the lines of chalk with toilet paper.

6. Students may also add blended chalk lines to create folds in the fabric of the tablecloth.

Paul Cézanne

Paul Cézanne (1839–1906) was one of the leading artists at the end of the nineteenth century. He is well known for his paintings of landscapes and still lifes. Cézanne worked hard to use color and value to give his paintings depth. He believed that using contrasting tones and colors made his drawings and paintings successful.

Literature References

Paul Cezanne (Getting to Know the World's Greatest Artists) by Mike Venezia; Children's Press, 1998.

Pattern Portraits

Materials

- example of a portrait by Henri Matisse (Try to find one that uses many patterns.)
- clothing and fabric with patterns
- vase with flowers
- table
- chair

For each student:

- drawing paper—white 11" x 17" (28 x 43 cm)
- pencil
- tempera paint—black and colors
- paintbrushes
- skin-tone oil pastels
- construction paper—black 12" x 18" (30.5 x 46 cm)
- glue

2, 3

4

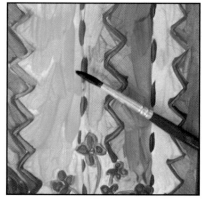

5

Art Elements

Line

Shape

Color

Talk About...

Talk about Matisse and his portraits. Have the students locate the patterns in the paintings. Talk about Matisse's travels and how he collected fabrics to use in his paintings. Ask the students if the person in the painting is drawn proportionally.

Step by Step

1. Set up a live still life with a chair, patterned fabric on the table, and a model from the class dressed in patterned clothes. Have students sketch the scene lightly in pencil on the white paper.

2. Using a thin brush and black paint, students trace the pencil lines. Let the paintings dry.

3. Students sketch in a patterned background behind the model.

4. Students paint in colorful patterns in the background and clothes, leaving the skin blank. Let the paintings dry.

5. Students fill in all skin areas with the skin-tone oil pastels.

6. Mount the paintings on black paper and display them for all to enjoy.

Henri Matisse

Henri Matisse (1869–1954) was born in France. He studied to be a lawyer and then became an artist at the age of 23. Matisse used a lot of patterns in his paintings. In his travels he collected patterned fabrics from different places and looked at them as he painted. Matisse liked to paint with expressive lines and forms. His paintings are colorful and full of energy.

Literature References

A Bird or Two: A Story About Henri Matisse by Bijou Le Tord; Wm. B. Eerdmans Publishing Co., 1999.

Matisse (Famous Artists) by Antony Mason, Andrew S. Hughes, and Jen Green; Barron's Juveniles, 1995.

Musician Collages

Materials

- photograph of Pablo Picasso's *Three Musicians*

For each student:

- scraps of wallpaper and wrapping paper
- construction paper—

  black 12" x 18"
  (30.5 x 46 cm)

  green 11" x 17"
  (28 x 43 cm)

  scraps of black, white, and assorted colors

- scissors
- glue
- black permanent marking pen
- scraps of gold foil paper

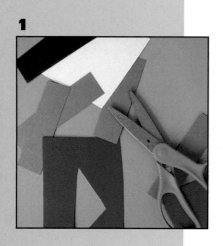

1

2

3

Art Elements

Line

Shape

Color

Texture

Talk About...

Show students a photograph of Picasso's *Three Musicians*. Ask the students to find the three musicians and their instruments. Ask:

• What do you notice about the people?

• Are they realistic or stylized?

• What kinds of shapes do you see?

Step by Step

1. Using the scraps of paper, students cut out shapes to make their musicians. They should give their musicians a hat like the musicians in the painting and use patterned paper for their clothes. Encourage students to use mostly squares and rectangles.

2. Students arrange the shapes to create their musicians on the green paper. Once they are happy with their layouts, they glue the shapes in place.

3. Have each student choose an instrument their musician will play. Using the gold foil paper, students cut out the instrument and glue it in place.

4. Students add details with a permanent black marker.

5. Mount the pictures on black paper and share them with the class.

Pablo Picasso

Pablo Picasso was born in Spain in 1881 and died in France in 1973. Picasso was always shocking people with his artwork. His painting style changed more over the period of his life than that of any other great artist. He helped invent a kind of art called Cubism. A lot of his paintings look like he has broken the object he was painting into blocks or cubes. He was also one of the first artists to use a collage technique by adding in different objects to his paintings.

Literature References

Picasso (Famous Children) by Tony Hart; Barron's Juveniles, 1994.

Picasso and the Girl with a Ponytail: A Story About Pablo Picasso by Laurence Anholt; Barron's Juveniles, 1998.

Black-and-White Pottery

Materials

- photos of black-and-white pottery found in Anasazi ruins
- kiln, oven, or place to dry the pots
- examples of designs from Anasazi pottery

For each student:

- white clay (Depending on your facilities, you may use real clay, oven-bake clay, or air-drying clay.)
- pencil
- newsprint
- black marking pen
- thin paintbrush
- black acrylic paint

1

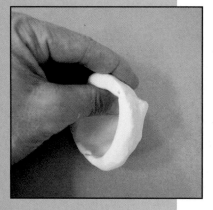

2

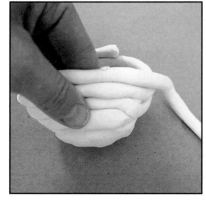

5

Art Elements

Line

Shape

Texture

Form

Talk About...

Talk about the Anasazi culture. Show pictures of their cliff dwellings and pottery. Have the students look for the elements of art that are included in their pottery designs.

Step by Step

1. Students form pinch pots.

   • Give each student a piece of clay.
   • Students make a ball that is about the size of a golf ball.
   • Students put the ball on the end of their thumb, being careful not to push the thumb through the clay. They begin pinching the ball between thumb and other fingers. The ball is rotated as it is pinched until a bowl is formed.

2. Students add coils to the pinch pot.

   • Have students take a bit more clay and roll it into a 1/2"-wide (1.5 cm) coil.
   • Attach the coil to the top rim of the pinch pot. (If you are using regular clay, students will need to slip and score both areas to stick them together.)
   • Blend in the coil to the top rim of the pot.
   • Students may add as many coils as they want.
   • Students write their names with a pencil on the bottom of their pots.

3. Let the pots dry according to clay manufacturer's directions.

4. Talk to the students about the designs on Anasazi pottery. Show examples. Have students practice making some geometric designs with a black marker on the newsprint.

5. Once the pots are dry, students use thin brushes and black tempera paint to paint on their chosen design.

Anasazi Peoples

The Anasazi peoples lived in the Southwest of the United States. They are remembered for their homes built into the cliffs. The Anasazi peoples are the ancestors of the Pueblo Indians who now live in New Mexico. About AD 900, Anasazi artists began making their well-known black-and-white pottery. It has intricate geometric designs similar to the woven designs of their baskets. This pottery was formed using a coil technique. When the pottery was leather hard, it would be burnished with a smooth polishing stone. Once the pottery was polished, the geometric designs were painted on using a brush made out of yucca leaves. The "paint" was a bee-plant extract. The pottery was then pit-fired, which turned the painted areas black while the unpainted areas remained white.

Literature References

Anasazi by Leonard Everett Fisher; Atheneum, 1997.

The Anasazi (New True Books) by David Petersen; Children's Press, 1991.

Tessellations

Materials

- examples of M.C. Escher's tessellations

For each student:

- tagboard or thick paper—3" (7.5 cm) square
- scissors
- tape
- crayons and colored pencils
- pencil
- practice paper
- white paper—9" x 12" (23 x 30.5 cm)
- black fine-point marking pen

1

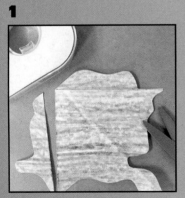

3

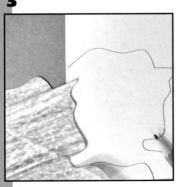

4

5

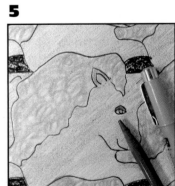

Art Elements

Line

Shape

Color

Talk About...

The word *tessellation* comes from *tessella*, which is a small stone or tile used in Roman mosaics. We can find tessellations everywhere around us in tile, wallpaper, and fabric designs.

Talk about M.C. Escher and his artwork. Discuss tessellations. Look for examples of tessellation around the room.

Step by Step

1. Students make a template shape from the tagboard square.

   - Use a crayon to color one side of the square. The other side is left white. Use the colored side.
   - Starting at the upper left corner and ending at the lower left corner of the same side, cut an interesting line.
   - Slide the cut piece straight across the square and tape it on the opposite side.
   - Using the same technique, cut a line from the bottom left corner to the bottom right corner.
   - Slide the piece straight up and tape it on the top of the square.

2. Ask students to decide what this shape will be. Will it be an animal, an object, or just a design? They are to lightly pencil in the defining lines on the template.

3. Students begin tracing the template onto the white paper. They place the template in the bottom left corner of the paper and trace carefully around it. Then they move the template to the right and fit it into the edge of the first tracing. There should be no gaps. They will continue to trace and move the template until they fill the entire paper with their shape.

4. Students draw in pencil the details inside their shape. The sample shape has been made into a horse. Students then carefully trace over their pencil lines with a black fine-point marking pen.

5. Students use crayons or colored pencils to color their tessellation.

M.C. Escher

Maurits Cornelius Escher was born in the Netherlands in 1898 and died in 1972. His interest in tessellation developed after seeing a tile floor in Spain in 1936. He worked to animate the tessellating shapes instead of working with abstract geometrical designs. Escher incorporated his animated tessellation into his woodcuts and lithographs.

Literature References

The M.C. Escher Coloring Book: 24 Images to Color by M.C. Escher; Harry N. Abrams, 1995.

M.C. Escher: His Life and Complete Graphic Work by M.C. Escher; Harry N. Abrams, 1992.

The M.C. Escher Sticker Book: 79 Imaginative Stickers by M.C. Escher; Harry N. Abrams, 1995.

Pop Art Sculptures

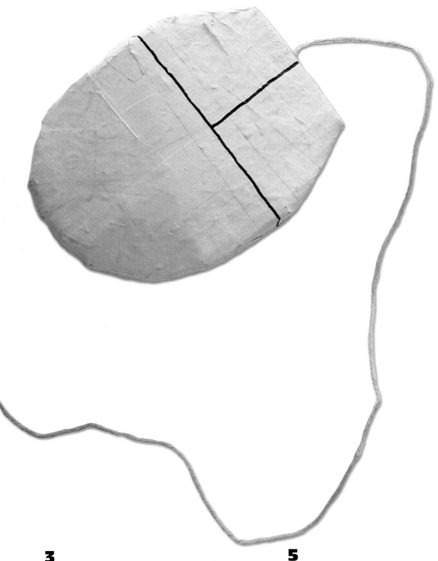

Materials

- pictures of Claes Oldenburg's sculptures

For each student (or group):

- practice paper to sketch ideas on
- pencil
- boxes, balloons, paper tubes, and other objects to help create a base for sculpture
- tagboard or cardboard
- scissors
- tape
- newspaper torn in strips
- papier-mâché paste
- bowl
- tempera paint
- paintbrushes
- markers
- wire, aluminum foil, and string
- glue

2

3

5

Art Elements

Shape

Color

Form

Texture

Talk About...

Show the pictures of Claes Oldenburg's sculptures and talk about Pop Art. Ask the students what objects they think a pop artist would choose to represent today. Have the students look around the room to find an ordinary object they would like to make into a large sculpture. (You may want to break the class into groups if you want several students to work on one sculpture. Several hands will probably be more helpful.)

Step by Step

1. Have each student, or group, choose an object and make a drawing of it.

2. Students make the basic form of the object using boxes, balloons or tubes, and tape.

3. Students cover their object with newspaper strips dipped in the papier-mâché paste.

4. Let the sculpture dry completely.

5. Students paint their sculptures.

   • First paint the entire sculpture with the main color of their object.
   • Let the paint dry.
   • Then paint or use a marker to add any details.
   • Add any extra objects for detail.

6. Display the Pop Art sculptures.

Claes Oldenburg

Claes Oldenburg, born in 1929, is one of Pop Art's creative artists. Pop Art became popular during the late 1960s. Pop artists took familiar objects from society and made a statement about them by including these regular objects in their artwork. Oldenburg is well known for his larger-than-life sculptures of everyday objects. He made a giant hamburger that is six feet wide and a bag of shoestring potatoes that is nine feet tall. Oldenburg first makes a life-size model, sculpts the large object out of fabric, and then paints it. Other objects included in his sculptures are the telephone, scissors, an ice bag, and a large spoon with a cherry on it. These ordinary objects became extraordinary sculptures.

Literature References

The American Eye: Eleven Artists of the Twentieth Century by Jan Greenberg; Delacorte Press, 1995.

Claes Oldenburg, Coosje Van Bruggen edited by Germano Celant; Skira, 1999.

Printed Stuff: Prints, Posters, and Ephemera by Claes Oldenburg: A Catalogue Raisonne 1958–1996 by Richard H. Axsom; Hudson Hills Press, 1997.

Bark Paintings

Materials

- example of Aboriginal bark paintings

For each student:

- brown paper grocery bags
- construction paper—brown 12" x 18" (30.5 x 46 cm)
- pencil
- scissors
- glue
- colored chalk
- toilet paper
- oil pastels—tan, brown, white, yellow, red, and black

1, 2

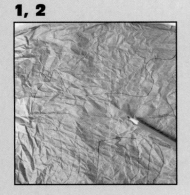

3

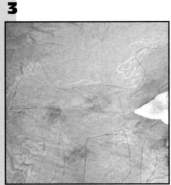

4, 5

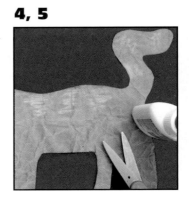

6

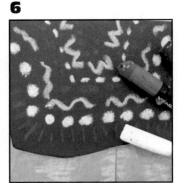

Art Elements

Line

Shape

Color

Value

Texture

Talk About...

Talk about Aboriginal bark paintings. Show some examples and have the students notice the use of circles and dots.

Step by Step

1. Students cut out the front or back panel of a grocery bag. They prepare their "bark" by crumpling and uncrumpling it several times.

2. On the bark, students make a pencil outline (contour) drawing of the animal they would like to have in their painting.

3. Students lightly rub their choice of chalk onto their animal to fill the entire shape. Blend the chalk into the paper with a piece of toilet paper.

4. Students cut out their animal along the lines of their pencil drawing and glue it in the center of the brown construction paper.

5. Using oil pastels, students add details to their animals.

6. Talk about lines and circles. Have students think about how lines can symbolize feelings or characteristics such as loud, soft, nice, or mean. List examples on the board for reference. Students decide what feeling they want to express about their animals. Using lines and circles that express that feeling, they make a design around the animal with oil pastels. For example, a picture of a grizzly bear might be surrounded by zigzag lines representing its growl. A snake might be surrounded by wavy lines representing the way it moves. Students completely fill the areas around the animal with patterns of lines and circles.

Australian Aborigines

The Aborigine peoples of Australia created an art form called bark painting. Originally these paintings were not meant to be a work of art, but rather a form of communication. The paintings were created to tell stories. A distinctive quality of these bark paintings is the use of repetitive dots and circles. Pigments from natural sources like plants were painted on the bark of the eucalyptus tree. The pigments were usually brown, white, tan, yellow, red, and black. Contemporary art from Australia includes acrylic paints instead of the natural pigments.

Literature References

Aboriginal Art of Australia: Exploring Cultural Traditions (Art Around the World) by Carol Finley; Lerner Publications Company, 1999.

Dreamings: The Art of Aboriginal Australia by Peter Sutton; George Braziller, 1997.

Mosaics

Materials

- photographs of mosaics

For each student:

- construction paper—black
  9" x 12" (23 x 30.5 cm)
- paper scraps and magazine
  pages cut into small squares
- glue or glue stick
- pencil

2

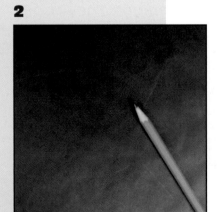

3

4

Art Elements

Shape

Color

Value

Texture

Space

Talk About...

Show examples of mosaics. Ask students if they have seen any simple mosaics in their home (tile counters or showers). Of course, the mosaics we find in our homes are much simpler than the mosaics created during the Middle Ages. The Romans used brilliant colors of glass to create their mosaics.

Step by Step

1. Students pick a topic for their mosaic. It could be an animal, a person, or a simple design.

2. Students lightly sketch their chosen design on the black paper.

3. Students choose the colors of cut paper squares they need for their picture. They lay out the paper squares on the black paper to create their image. Encourage them to leave a black border around each tile to represent the mortar that holds all the pieces together in a real mosaic. Students can use their knowledge of value and placement to create space in their pictures.

4. Once the images are laid out as desired, the students glue their pieces in place.

Roman Tile Workers

Mosaics are created by using different-colored tiles to make an image. The tiles are usually laid in a mortar to keep them in place. They were used by the Romans to decorate their cathedrals and churches. The tiles used included bits of glass, stone, and gold. Often the subject matter focused on religious and political images because that was what was important to the people of the Roman culture.

Literature References

Amazing Mosaics by Sarah Kelly; Barron's Juveniles, 2000.

Geometric Patterns from Roman Mosaics by Robert Field; Parkwest Publications, 1993.

Mosaics of the Greek and Roman World by Katherine M. D. Dunbabin; Cambridge University Press, 2000.

Flowers

Materials

- reproductions of Georgia O'Keefe's artwork

For each student:

- pictures of flowers from bulb catalogs
- white drawing paper— 18" x 24" (46 x 61 cm)
- pencil
- colored chalk
- toilet paper
- spray fixative

2

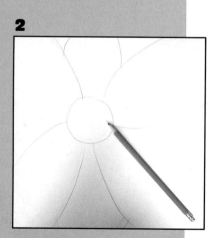

4

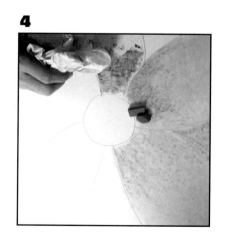

5

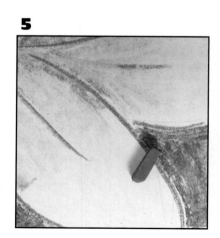

Art Elements

Line

Shape

Color

Value

Space

Talk About...

Talk about Georgia O'Keefe and show several pictures of her flower paintings. Ask:

• Do O'Keefe's flowers fill the page and touch the edges or are they small and in the center of the page?

• Did O'Keefe use one flower or a bunch of flowers?

• Do the flowers look real or abstract?

• How does she make the flowers look real?

Step by Step

1. After examining Georgia O'Keefe's flowers, let the students choose a picture of a flower they would like to create in her style. Perhaps they may look at pictures in a bulb catalog for inspiration.

2. Using a pencil VERY LIGHTLY, students draw one flower to fill the entire paper. The drawing must touch all four sides of the paper. Point out to the students that by drawing their flower, they are using line and shape.

3. Demonstrate how to use the colored chalk lightly in some areas and darker in other areas to create space in the flower. Inside the flower will be darker, while the outer areas of the petals that are in the light will be lighter. Use a bit of the toilet paper to lightly blend the chalk. By using different values, students will create space in their drawings.

4. Students add color to their flowers with the colored chalk.

5. Once the flowers are completed, have the students name their flower's predominant color. Then they choose the complementary color from the color wheel to fill in the background.

6. Spray the drawings with spray fixative to set the chalk and then display the beautiful flowers.

Georgia O'Keefe

Georgia O'Keefe (1887–1986) is one of America's greatest painters. She was born in Wisconsin in 1887. At the age of twelve, Georgia's mother signed her up for painting lessons. Georgia decided to become an artist. She wanted to create art that was personal and expressed her feelings. Later on, Georgia moved to New York to go to art school. In 1924 she began to paint flowers. She painted them big and colorful so that the busy New Yorkers would stop and take time to look at them.

Literature References

The Georgia O'Keefe Museum by Peter H. Hassrick; Harry N. Abrams, 1997.

Georgia O'Keefe—Selected Works: Prints/With Teacher's Guide; Modern Learning Press, 1993.

Portrait of an Artist: A Biography of Georgia O'Keefe by Laurie Lisle; Washington Square Press, 1997.

Pop Art Food Posters

Materials

- examples of artwork by Andy Warhol and Roy Lichtenstein

For each student:

- construction paper—white 9" x 12" (23 x 30.5 cm)
- pencil
- marking pens—

  black permanent fine-tipped pen

  assorted colors of watercolor pens
- ruler

1, 2

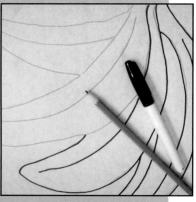

3

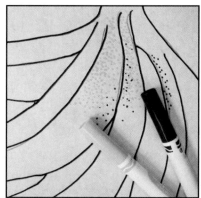

4

Art Elements

Line

Shape

Color

Value

Texture

Talk About...

Show the examples of artwork by Andy Warhol and Roy Lichtenstein. Ask students what images these artists might use if they were taking popular items from today's culture.

Talk about the dots in Lichtenstein's artwork. Have the students practice making dots with the tips of the colored markers on a piece of practice paper. Notice that the dots close together give a darker value than the dots placed farther apart. When two colors of dots are mixed, the colors change.

Step by Step

1. Have each student choose a food item. They make a contour line drawing (outside line only, no fill or shading) of their food in pencil on the white paper. The food item should fill the page.

2. Students trace over their pencil lines with fine-tipped black markers.

3. Using dots made with the tips of markers, students add color to their drawings. They must use dots! They can create value by using the dots close together or far apart and can mix dots to create different colors. They can also use dots in different ways to give their food texture.

4. Have the students pick one or two colors that contrast with their food. Using a ruler, students draw stripes to fill in the background.

5. Students sign their artwork and then display it!

Andy Warhol and Roy Lichtenstein

In the 1960s, Pop Art became popular. Pop artists used items that were familiar and made a statement about them. Two of the most famous Pop artists were Andy Warhol and Roy Lichtenstein. Andy Warhol used a photo silk-screening process to put images from the media onto his large canvases. He is known for his repeated use of the same image. Some of his most famous works show Marilyn Monroe, Elvis, Campbell's soup cans, and money. Roy Lichtenstein painted his images in the style of a comic strip. His paintings are made up of dots to imitate the "Benday" dots used to mass print images in books and papers.

Literature References

Andy Warhol (Essential Series) by Ingrid Schaffner; Andrews McMeel Publishing, 1999.

Andy Warhol (Getting to Know the World's Greatest Artists) by Mike Venezia; Children's Press, 1997.

Roy Lichtenstein's ABC by Bob Adelman; Bullfinch Press, 1999.

Roy Lichtenstein (Basic Series) by Janis Hendrickson; TASCHEN America Llc., 1996.

Self-Portraits

Materials

- examples of self-portraits by Vincent Van Gogh

For each student:

- tagboard or thick paper— two 12" x 14" (30.5 x 35.5 cm)
- pencil
- black fine-tipped permanent marking pen
- hand mirror
- paintbrush
- foam egg carton
- thick tempera paint—Mix 1 tablespoon of cornstarch or flour with each 1/2 cup of paint. Paint colors are needed for skin tones, hair, eye, lip, and clothing colors.
- torn bits of colored tissue paper
- white glue
- scissors

1

2, 3

5

6

Art Elements

Line

Shape

Color

Texture

Talk About...

Show the examples of Vincent Van Gogh's self-portraits. Ask the students to notice his use of thick paint and explain the term *impasto*. Ask students to notice Van Gogh's expression, his position, and the texture created by the impasto.

Step by Step

1. Each student starts with a piece of the thick paper or tagboard. Have them look in a mirror and use a pencil to draw themselves from the shoulders up. They need to fill the page! Make sure their bodies go off the bottom of the paper and that their heads almost touch the top of the paper.

2. Using a paintbrush, the students apply thickened paint to their faces, eyes, lips, hair, and clothes on the self-portrait to give it a more textured look. Let the paint dry.

3. Students trace over the portrait lines with the black marking pen.

4. Students cut out the self-portraits.

5. Using watered-down glue and a brush, students cover a second sheet of paper with torn tissue paper bits. The pieces should overlap one another. Suggest that students pick a color family (warm or cool) and keep their background in that family.

6. When the tissue paper is dry, students glue their self-portraits onto the background.

7. Students sign their artwork and it is ready for display!

Vincent Van Gogh

Vincent Van Gogh was not well known during his lifetime, but he is now known as one of the world's greatest artists. Vincent was a sad man and did not smile in his self-portraits, though he painted several of them. During his painting career, Van Gogh sold one painting for $80. Today his paintings, using thick paint and colors straight out of the tube, are worth millions. This thick or heavy use of paint showing the marks of the brush is known as *Impasto*. Vincent Van Gogh used impasto to add feelings and emotions in his paintings.

Literature References

Camille and the Sunflowers: A Story About Vincent Van Gogh by Laurence Anholt; Barron's Juveniles, 1994.

The First Starry Night by Joan Shaddox Isom; Charlesbridge Publishing, 1998.

Painting the Wind by Michelle Dionetti; Little, Brown and Company Inc., 1996.

Van Gogh (Basic Art) edited by Taschen; TASCHEN America Llc., 2000.

Rock Art

Materials

- visual examples of pictographs and petroglyphs
- examples of symbols used in rock art

For each student:

- thick paper or thin tagboard—
  4" x 6" (10 x 15 cm)
- pencil
- masking tape
- construction paper—brown
  9" x 12" (23 x 30.5 cm)
- brayer
- black or brown printing ink
- oil pastels—brown, yellow, red, beige, gray, white

1, 2

4

7

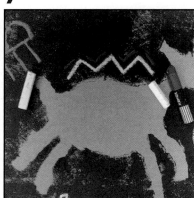

Art Elements

Line

Shape

Texture

Talk About...

Discuss rock art with students and show them the examples. Ask them if they can tell the difference between two different types of rock art. Talk about *petroglyphs* and *pictographs*. Also talk about the images on the rocks. Many of the symbols are simply made out of lines and shapes.

Step by Step

1. Give each student a piece of thick paper or tagboard. Have them draw the outline of an animal of their choice in pencil. This is a contour drawing. There should not be any details!

2. Students carefully tear out their animal along the pencil line. This torn animal is a stencil.

3. With a small piece of masking tape, students attach their animal stencils to the center of the brown paper.

4. Students roll an even amount of brown or black ink onto the paper with a brayer. The entire paper should be covered. The animal stencil will keep the ink from covering that part.

5. Let the papers dry.

6. Talk again about petroglyphs and pictographs. The painted papers represent petroglyphs, because the animal drawings are "carved" into the painted paper. Now have students add pictographs to their designs.

7. Students use the oil pastels to add pictographs on the inked area of their paper.

Prehistoric Peoples

Humans have communicated in one way or another throughout history. One way we communicate is by writing symbols or drawing pictures. Rock art is an example of how prehistoric people communicated and recorded their lives. There are two different types of rock art. **Petroglyphs** are carved into the rock. **Pictographs** are drawn or painted on the surface of the rock.

Literature References

Native American Rock Art: Messages from the Past by Yvette La Pierre; Lickle Publishing Inc., 1994.

Stories in Stone: Rock Art Pictures by Early Americans by Caroline Arnold; Clarion Books, 1996.

Gargoyles

Materials

- photographs and pictures of gargoyles and Gothic architecture

For each student:

- clay
- texture tools (nails, craft sticks, toothpicks, etc.)
- gray tempera paint
- paintbrush

1

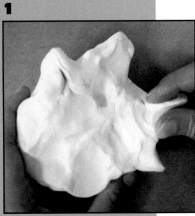

2

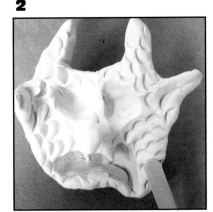

6

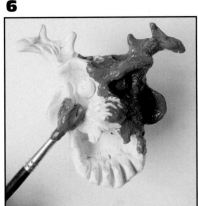

Art Elements

Form

Texture

Talk About...

Talk about gargoyles with students. Show pictures of Gothic architecture and gargoyles.

Step by Step

1. Help students make gargoyles using a pinch-pull technique. Start each student off with a block or ball of clay. Keeping the clay all in one piece, students use their fingers to pull and pinch the clay into a creature. They might want to pull out legs, wings, and a head.

2. Students should experiment with texture tools to press in and draw details on the basic gargoyle form. The head of a nail or the rounded end of a wooden craft stick makes good scales when pressed in repeatedly.

3. Students hollow out the bottom of their gargoyles so they can dry more quickly.

4. Students add their names to the bottom of their gargoyles.

5. Let the clay dry and then fire or bake according to the clay manufacturer's directions.

6. Students paint their gargoyles gray to make them look like stone.

Medieval Architects and Builders

Medieval architects and builders included ornate gargoyles as part of the buildings they designed and built. Gargoyles are stone figures found mainly on the top of Gothic-style buildings. Because they were originally used as drains on castles and churches, the gargoyles' mouths were usually open. Gargoyles were also believed to scare off evil spirits from the buildings they were placed upon. They fit in well with the ornate decoration of the time. Usually, gargoyles are in the form of made-up creatures.

Literature References

Gargoyles: 30 Postcards; Abbeville Press, Inc., 1999.

God Bless the Gargoyles by Dav Pilkey; Voyager Picture Book, 1996.

Holy Terrors: Gargoyles on Medieval Buildings by Janetta Rebold Benton; Abbeville Press, Inc., 1997.

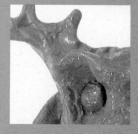

- **Variety of papers**
  - colored construction paper— full-sized sheets, scraps
  - paper bags
  - tissue and toilet paper
  - wallpaper
  - wrapping paper
  - cardboard
  - newspaper
  - magazines
  - tagboard
- **Variety of craft supplies**
  - straws
  - pipe cleaners
  - craft sticks
  - string
  - yarn
  - material scraps
  - buttons
  - dried beans
- **Artists' tools**
  - scissors
  - paste
  - glue
  - stapler
  - tape
  - hole punch
  - brushes
  - rulers
- **Painting supplies**
  - tempera paint in assorted colors
  - watercolor trays
  - sponges for printing
  - gadgets for printing
  - trays or plates for mixing new colors
- **Reference materials**
  - color wheel
  - samples of fine art
  - literature with illustrations that reflect a certain style
- **Job cards**
  - challenges
  - directions for specific projects

An Art Center in Your Classroom

Many of the activities in this book can be done as center activities. Create an area of your classroom that can be designated as the art center. Include a table and an easel for working, materials, and a drying area. Think about access to a sink for easy cleanup. You may also want to include an oversized trash can, plastic covers for the table, and plastic drop cloths for carpeted areas.

Space for displaying student art can be a big problem. Suspend a narrow clothesline between two ladders. Hang a container of clothespins on one rung. You are ready for hanging papers! Your gallery can double as a drying place. Hang pictures back to back to increase space.